Flh
30

P!
0.
3
q

PRICE

D1320237

RESERVE STOCK

PLEASE APPLY TO STAFF

HENRY IV

HENRY IV

Bryan Bevan

THE RUBICON PRESS

The Rubicon Press
57 Cornwall Gardens
London SW7 4BE

British Library Cataloguing in Publication Data

Bevan, Bryan
Henry IV
I. Title
942.041092

ISBN 0-948695-35-8
ISBN 0-948695-36-6 pbk

Designed and typeset by The Rubicon Press
Printed and bound in Great Britain by Biddles Limited of Guildford
and King's Lynn

For my sister Win

Contents

List of Illustrations

Acknowledgements

To the Tustees and Mr J. Conway, Superintendent Manuscripts Collections, and Staff of the British Library for their help.

To the National Library of Wales for their valuable assistance when I was researching the Anglo-Welsh War.

To the London Library as always for letting me keep borrowed books long after the permitted period.

To my sister Win Murray and Andrew Low for accompanying me on a memorable journey to visit Castles in North and South Wales.

To my publishers Anthea Page and Juanita Homan for suggesting the idea of the book and for their constant encouragement.

To Ann Holland for her encouragement.

To Mr Joseph Cooke for kindly showing me Lincoln's historic Stonebow and Guildhall.

To Sadika Tancred for her help.

I   Henry of Bolingbroke

Henry Bolingbroke was a child of the medieval age, a time of violent contrasts, far more passionate than today. The contrasts between suffering and joy, between despair and happiness were much more marked. Disasters struck with a greater impact, while honours and riches bestowed on the few were sharply emphasized in the abject poverty of the many. Life was full of cruel ostentation, the leper rattling his chains, the beggar taking a hideous pleasure in exhibiting his deformity. Executions were in public, a dire warning for the evildoers. Everything was devised to arouse coarse emotions, and excessive excitement among the people. Refinements of torture were invented to prolong the agony of the criminal, and grand spectacles and pageants were staged in which the victim, the judge, the executioner and the people all played an elaborate part.

In his fine book *The Waning of the Middle Ages*, J. Huisinga dwells on "the despair and distracted joy, between cruelty and pious tenderness which characterise life in the Middle Ages". One thing so sadly lacking today, but prevalent in the Middle Ages, was the sweet chiming of bells now summoning the citizen to prayer, now warning him of danger, and calling upon him to mourn or to rejoice. We pride ourselves today on our ancient traditions, on the beauty and precision of our pageants, but during medieval times the entry of princes was also arranged with every resource available at the time. While life was to be enjoyed, many were increasingly obsessed with death and were fearful of it, particularly after 1348, when the Black Death reached its zenith. Yet with all its harshness and brutality, there still existed the longing of the pious pilgrim to trudge to Jerusalem. And Henry Bolingbroke, as a gallant knight, possessing chivalrous ideals, was typical of his age in his desire to lead a crusade to recover Jerusalem from the Infidel.

      *   *   *   *

Henry was born at Bolingbroke Castle on the southern tip of the Lincolnshire wolds about April 1366, thus nine months older than his first cousin Richard of Bordeaux, the future Richard II. The date is actually uncertain because in the fourteenth century no great trouble was taken to record the birthdays of members of the royal house. It is possible that he was born during 1367, since in the summer or autumn of this year two messengers bringing news of the birth were separately rewarded by the infant's paternal grandfather King Edward III and his eldest son, the Black Prince. However, this might refer to another birth, that of an infant son of the Duchess Blanche, who did not survive. Bolingbroke Castle was an impressive fortress, built during the reign of King Stephen in the 1130s, and attached to the earldom of Lincoln, a title held by John of Gaunt, Henry's father, in right of his first wife Blanche, Duchess of Lancaster. Bolingbroke with its four towers and prisons, was the chief seat of the duchy where all the records were jealously preserved.[1] Today the village is still medieval.

John of Gaunt's marriage to Blanche of Lancaster, a great heiress in 1359, was one of the brilliant marriages arranged by his father Edward III for his fourth son, who was nineteen. Proud, arrogant and ambitious, John of Gaunt (born at Ghent in 1340) was to exercise a powerful influence over his only surviving son Henry. His mother, the Lady Blanche, an enchanting personality, was the younger daughter of Henry of Grosmont, Duke of Lancaster, a great-grandson of Henry III. Little is known of this magnate, but he was a close confidant and friend of Edward III, his cousin, and a brilliant soldier during the earlier part of the Hundred Years' War, well versed in diplomacy. Despite his ability, he was a strangely humble man, possessing the adventurous and devout spirit of a Crusader. To wander in the ancient village of Grosmont in Wales, so beautifully situated on the Monnow as it is today, and to imagine Henry of Grosmont sallying forth to hunt the deer in the park of his favourite castle, now a ruin, is a fascinating pastime.

When he died in 1361 he left two daughters, Maud and Blanche, both co-heiresses, for they now jointly inherited the many castles and lands of their father. Maud died early, leaving Blanche the sole heiress. Henry Bolingbroke hardly knew his mother, for she also died on September 12th 1369 when he was barely two - a victim of the dreaded plague. She was aged abut twenty-six. She comes alive so vividly in Geoffrey Chaucer's 'Boke of the Duchess', where she is described as "a lovely, gay noblewoman". He knew her well. "I saw her daunce so comily carole and singe so swetely laughe and playe so womanly and loke so debonairly..." Henry's father John of Gaunt, was desolate, but he was to make two more marriages.

John of Gaunt was the owner of over thirty castles and very much land, and one may think of him now as an overmighty subject. He owned, among others, Bolingbroke and Lincoln Castles, Hertford, Leicester, Dunstanburgh in Northumberland, Nottingham, Lancaster, Grosmont, Skenfrith, Monmouth and Kenilworth, one of his favourites, being proud of its barbaric grandeur and wonderful banqueting hall. His London homes included Savoy Palace, once his father-in-law's.

Henry Bolingbroke was especially fortunate in boyhood to have a father to guide him and advise him, unlike his cousin Richard, whose father, the Black Prince, died in 1376. Thus Bolingbroke was born in the purple, a nobleman of importance surrounded by retainers and household knights from an early age. Henry's nurse was Margaret Taaf of Dublin, and during 1369 Lady Wake, a daughter of an earlier Henry of Lancaster, was appointed and paid by John of Gaunt one hundred marks (£66.13s.4d) for looking after Henry and his entourage.[2] She lived mostly at Bourne Castle bordering the fens in Lincolnshire, thirty miles from the Lancastrian stronghold of Bolingbroke Castle. With Henry at Bourne Castle were his two younger sisters, Elizabeth and Philippa.

John of Gaunt, Shakespeare's "time-honoured Lancaster", was extremely ambitious, but his ambitions lay rather overseas than in England. His second marriage (1371) to the Spanish Princess Costanza (Constance), entirely political in its purpose, gave him the magnificent chance of being crowned beside her in the Cathedral of Burgos as the husband of the Queen of Castile and Leon. She was the daughter of Pedro the Cruel, ousted from his throne by his illegitimate half-brother Henry of Trastamare. Such a marriage of convenience was loveless, for Edward III's third surviving son[3] deeply loved his mistress of many years,

Katherine Swynford, the widow of a Lincolnshire knight, Sir Hugh Swynford. One suspects a proud Spaniard such as Princess Costanza would not have accepted her husband's adultery so meekly as has been suggested by contemporary chroniclers or modern historians.

Katherine Swynford had first entered the household of the Duchess Blanche as governess to her children. After her death Katherine became the mistress of John of Gaunt, who was a typical Plantagenet, like his father, in his love of women. She was indeed one of the outstanding women of her age, not only beautiful but deeply intelligent, a very capable manager and possessing infinite tact in her relations with Costanza of Castile. It was Katherine[4] who announced the birth of Costanza's only daughter to the old King Edward III in his dotage. It is curious that Katherine was the sister of Philippa Chaucer, wife of the poet Geoffrey Chaucer, and Philippa regularly attended Princess Costanza.[5]

When he was eight, Henry Bolingbroke had a male governor, Thomas de Burton, but Katherine was in charge of his sisters, Elizabeth and Philippa of Lancaster, for many years. She soon became the mother of John of Gaunt's three illegitimate sons, John, Henry and Thomas, who were given the name Beaufort after one of John of Gaunt's French estates.

All Henry's half-brothers were to have distinguished careers, especially Henry Beaufort. Katherine also had one daughter Joan by Gaunt, and had earlier produced by her husband, a legitimate son, Sir Thomas Swynford, a sinister character, destined to become a close companion of Henry Bolingbroke during his travels in Prussia. In 1396, two years after the death of Costanza, Gaunt married his third wife, Katherine Swynford,[6] in Lincoln Cathedral, and their Beaufort sons and daughter were legitimized by Richard II in an Act of Parliament a year later. It is in Lincoln and the surrounding country that memories of this brilliant woman still linger.

Henry Bolingbroke, a stocky little boy, his hair inclined to redness, became an accomplished youth, skilled in manners and etiquette, eager to be trained in jousting and venerye (hunting). He acquired an early interest in music, played the flute expertly and learnt to dance and sing. His father saw to it that Henry was well educated, taught to read and write in English and French, and to understand Latin.

His grandfather, the old King Edward III, remembering his disturbed youth, was all the more anxious that his grandson Richard, a boy scarcely ten years old, should succeed to his inheritance peaceably and without dispute. So, the benign old man in his dotage looked on, thinking perhaps of his own intimate friendship with Henry of Grosmont, first Duke of Lancaster, as he bestowed the Order of the Garter (the order of chivalry he had created) on Richard and Henry, aged ten and eleven. It was April 23rd 1377, St. George's Day, only two months before Edward's death at Sheen. During the ceremony they both swore an oath that they would never bear arms against one another, unless in the war of their liege lord, or in their own just quarrel. Who could have predicted then that Henry would depose his first cousin twenty-two years later! Both boys wore on this occasion a surcoat of white wool lined with blue with the blue garter prominently displayed containing its motto '*Honi soit qui mal y pense*'. Richard was fairer than Henry, possessing an almost feminine beauty. The chronicler Adam of Usk would later refer to him as 'beautiful as Absalom'.

On June 21st 1377, Edward died, after reigning fifty years, and bequeathed his grandson Richard a fearful inheritance. An uneasy peace might have reigned, but the admirals of France and Castile seized the opportunity to invade England's south coast, burning the little towns of Rye, Rottingdean and Hastings. The Scots were especially troublesome, making constant raids on Berwick-on-Tweed and the English borders.

At Richard's coronation on July 16th, his uncle John of Gaunt played a very prominent part, bearing the sword *Curtana,* the sword of mercy, but after High Mass, anxious that his son Henry should undertake important functions, delegated this duty to him. Henry was now known as Earl of Derby, one of his father's titles.

Already highly intelligent, Richard's mind was filled with a mystical sense of his role as king apart from others, but it is doubtful whether his devoted tutor, Sir Simon Burley or Nicholas Littlington,[7] the able Abbot of Westminster, were serving the King well by dwelling too much on royal absolutism. So exhausted was Richard by the coronation ritual that Simon Burley was forced to carry him out of the Abbey to Westminster Hall for the banquet. Henry probably despised his cousin for his lack of stamina.

After the coronation Richard remained very much in the care of his mother Princess Joan, the most beautiful woman of her age, according to Froissart. A government of regency had been formed, but it was ineffective, as members of the Council were unable to work harmoniously together. While the King was living at Kennington Palace during the autumn and winter of 1377, his cousin Henry shared the same tutor, Sir Simon Burley.

It was now that the seeds of mistrust were sown between the two boys. Not only were their tastes different, but their temperaments utterly dissimilar. Henry was more conventional than his cousin, excelling in such boyish sports as wrestling or duelling with toy swords. Richard was far less robust and could not compete in these activities. What, however, rankled with Henry was Richard's affection for Robert de Vere, Earl of Oxford, hereditary Great Chamberlain at Court, and five years Richard's senior. The boy king really loved de Vere, who was handsome, cultured and sophisticated, thus stirring up considerable resentment and jealousy in Henry. Whether in those early days there was a homosexual element in Richard's and de Vere's intimate friendship is open to question, but there is no evidence, although the chronicler Walsingham does hint at disgraceful behaviour.

De Vere took every opportunity to instil in Richard's mind that his uncle John of Gaunt, was plotting to usurp his throne, which was almost certainly untrue. During the last years of his father Edward III, the Duke of Lancaster had wielded great power, and was for some years, the most unpopular nobleman in the kingdom. Men murmured to each other in alehouses and in the marketplace that Gaunt had designs on the throne and even that he wished to poison his nephew. De Vere possibly had some reason for his opinion, but Bolingbroke naturally resented the unjustified attacks on his father, though it was less easy for him to defend his conduct when Bolingbroke openly sided with the Lords Appellant against their lawful king.

From the age of eleven until he was fifteen, Henry, Earl of Derby, mostly lived at one of his father's castles, Kenilworth, Leicester, Lincoln or Hertford, where he became skilled in jousting and other sports. His companions were his own sisters Philippa and Elizabeth, but it was a rather odd ménage, for it not only included his stepmother Costanza and her daughter Catalina, but his father's mistress Katherine Swynford, with her legitimate children Thomas and Blanche, and the various Beaufort brothers. His tutor, William Montendre, entered his service when Henry was about ten, and both Hugh Waterton, his Chamberlain or Keeper of the Wardrobe, and Hugh Herle, his Chaplain for nearly twenty years, were important members of his household. Waterton was a member of a family giving devoted service to the House of Lancaster, and they were to remain trusted friends after Henry became Duke of Lancaster and King of England.

John of Gaunt's choice of an heiress as a wife for his son was sagacious, though it made the House of Lancaster even more wealthy, over-powerful and rich in land. She was Mary, the younger daughter of Humphrey de Bohun, Earl of Hereford and Essex, hereditary Constable of England, who had died in 1373. The Bohuns were of Norman descent, originating from Bohon in Normandy.[8] After Humphrey's death, the vast Bohun inheritance was divided between her elder sister Alianor and herself. In July 1380 the marriage of Mary to his son Henry was bought from King Richard by John of Gaunt for 5000 marks, but the marriage was strongly opposed by the Duke of Lancaster's fiery youngest brother, Thomas of Woodstock, later Duke of Gloucester, and his wife Alianor. They attempted to send her to a convent, so that they could succeed to the whole inheritance, including Mary's Welsh estates. Gaunt managed to thwart their scheme. At the time of his first marriage Bolingbroke was fourteen, while Mary was three years younger.

It took place amidst scenes of considerable merriment at her mother, the Countess of Hereford's home, Rochford Hall, Essex. No expense was spared to make it a joyous affair, and two companies of minstrels sent by the boy king and Edmund of Langley, Gaunt's younger brother, enlivened the marriage festivities. There was a lavish banquet in Rochford Hall, while the minstrels played their airs. In medieval England there was plenty of fun, a Lord of Misrule dressed in a fool's costume, a-jingle with merry bells, to enhance the guests' enjoyment; there would be mummers disguised as bears and other animals to ride their hobby-horses through the great hall. For the bride it must have been a frightening event, sitting like a little shy leveret, but Henry's marriage to Mary was to be fruitful, if not happy, for she was to bear him four strong sons and two daughters.

For the present she was considered too young to cohabit with Henry, so she remained with her mother. However, within a few months she was pregnant, but their first son died in infancy.[9] One shared interest with Henry brought them close, their mutual love of music, for he would play the flute and she would sing in a sweet voice, and play a canticum. Later they seem to have been fond of chess. His marriage to Mary de Bohun was very advantageous to him, for he obtained among other lands the castles of Brecon in Wales, another in Hay in Herefordshire, and various land in Gloucestershire, Wiltshire and Hertfordshire.

1381 is one of the most important dates in the social history of England, when the Peasants' Revolt erupted. It concerns the biography of the boy king Richard II, rather than that of Henry of Bolingbroke, and Richard, as often related, showed indomitable courage in dealing with the rebels.

Henry also faced deadly perils while remaining in St. John's Chapel in the White Tower of the Tower of London, an exquisite example of Norman ecclesiastical architecture. Simon Sudbury, Archbishop of Canterbury, whilst holding High Mass before the altar, was seized by the bestial rabble and executed on Tower Green. Had it not been for John Ferrour of Southwark, Henry would have been murdered in St. John's Chapel, but his motives in saving Bolingbroke's life are unknown and have baffled historians. Henry did not lack gratitude, for nineteen years later, when Ferrour was tried for treason in Oxford Castle (1400), he was granted a free pardon.

John of Gaunt was away in Scotland during the Peasants' Revolt, which was fortunate for him. He was much hated by the people, who destroyed his magnificent Palace of the Savoy standing on the Thames between London and Westminster.

Richard II was a year older than his cousin Henry when he married Anne of Bohemia, daughter of the Holy Roman Emperor Charles IV, in St. Stephen's Chapel, Westminster Palace. It was a very happy marriage, though childless. It was young Henry Bolingbroke and his sister Elizabeth of Lancaster, who welcomed Anne outside London, accompanying Richard's queen on horseback over London Bridge and through East Cheap and through streets with fountains that spouted wine.[10] At Anne's coronation in Westminster Abbey on January 24th 1382, Henry was dressed splendidly in a gown of gold cloth of damask, beneath a cloak of satin, the gold leopards of England prominently displayed. This gown was a present from Costanza, Henry's stepmother. During the celebrations afterwards, he made a favourable impression with his skill in jousting in a tournament. His early popularity among the people was enhanced by his gallantry when twenty at the jousts held at Smithfield.

The distribution of Maundy money, nowadays only performed by the sovereign, was in medieval times also carried out by noblemen. We hear of Henry, Earl of Derby, on April 3rd 1382, at Hertford Castle, personally washing the feet of fifteen poor men and giving alms to each of them.

The beautiful city of Lincoln has intimate associations with both John of Gaunt and his son Henry. It was here while staying at Lincoln Castle that both were present at a trial before the bishop in the Cathedral of William Swinderby, a Lollard and follower of the great religious reformer John Wycliffe. Earlier John of Gaunt was reputed to have held Lollard sympathies, but he evidently approved on this occasion when Swinderby was found guilty. Four years later, on February 9th 1386 Henry, together with Thomas Swynford and Philippa Chaucer (wife of the poet), were admitted to the fraternity of Lincoln Cathedral,[11] thus enabling them to benefit from the spiritual rites celebrated there.

In his early life and indeed in his later life as king, Henry was always on the move with his itinerant household. In his restless peregrinations he visited all the Lancastrian castles, such as Leicester, Lincoln, Kenilworth and Pontefract, for it was essential as a great nobleman to make himself known to his tenants. One reason for this constant movement was the primitive sanitation in medieval times. In Hugh Waterton's Chamber account during 1381-3, 'horses' was the most expensive item. Such journeys required enormous organization. Heralds were often sent ahead to announce a great lord's arrival and to seek out lodgings. In the rear of the procession were carts full of baggage, including beds.

Later Henry, Earl of Derby, was to become a much travelled nobleman, but his first recorded journey overseas was during January 1383-4 together with his father, when they went to Calais to negotiate with Flanders. His first military experience was acquired in 1384 when he accompanied his father during his campaign against the Scots.

As he grew to manhood, Henry was an extrovert at least in his early life, popular with the people because of his affability, fondness for sport and love of jousting. For most of his forty-seven years, he was a handsome man, strong and stocky, with fine teeth, but not tall. He sported a thick beard of deep auburn. His pleasing manners and liberality endeared him to most people. He was devout and orthodox, free from any taint of his father's anticlericalism.[12] Where his cousin Richard possessed a strong imaginative sense, Henry lacked ingenuity. Rather he was calculating, cunning and opportunist, qualities much needed when he seized Richard's throne.

Robert de Vere continued to intrigue against John of Gaunt, much to the resentment of his son Henry Bolingbroke. During a Parliament held at Salisbury during 1384, de Vere almost certainly persuaded a Carmelite friar named John Latemar to fabricate a treasonable plot against Richard by John of Gaunt. The boy king, a typical Plantagenet in his passionate temper, was hard to restrain. To order his uncle to be put to death without calmly and thoroughly looking into the affair was extremely rash, if this is to be believed. The Duke of Lancaster protested his innocence so vigorously that the King was convinced of it. The friar, however, was subjected to brutal tortures from which he did not recover, although Richard is reputed to have shed many bitter tears.

During the Christmas festivities of 1384, there was a further plot against Henry's father, occasioned by a dispute on foreign affairs. Seemingly both de Vere, Earl of Oxford, and Thomas Mowbray, another friend of Richard's were plotting John of Gaunt's downfall or even murder. He wisely absented himself from a Council at Waltham, but goaded beyond endurance and wearing chain-mail under his clothes, went to Richard's Palace of Sheen accompanied by an escort. Boldly confronting his nephew, he refused to collaborate further until Richard reformed. The King's mother, Princess Joan, wisely intervened and a reconciliation was effected.[13]

Both the Duke of Lancaster and Robert de Vere accompanied Richard on his campaign against Scotland in 1385, but the favourite succeeded in preventing any reconciliation between the King and his uncle. He even insinuated that the Duke of Lancaster aspired to be king and hoped that Richard would be killed in the moorlands of Scotland. This antagonism between uncle and nephew at this period was unfortunate, for Richard sorely needed Gaunt's support in his imminent fight with his disloyal barons.

Now a dramatic event, the Battle at Aljubarotta, occurred during August 1385 when Portugal, under a Regent, who was soon to ascend the throne as King John (João) I, defeated the Spaniards under King Juan I. It was to affect the fortunes of both Henry and his father. In July 1386 John of Gaunt, Duke of Lancaster was at Plymouth with his family, eager to set sail for Spain and at last assert his claim through his wife Costanza to Castile and Leon. Henry rode to Plymouth to say farewell to his father, stepmother and his sisters. During his sojourn he stayed in his father's palace, the house of the friar's Carmelites, and there on June 16th he gave evidence among others, including his future enemy Owain Glyn Dŵr, in the celebrated heraldic dispute between Lord Scrope of Bolton and Robert Grosvenor of Hulme, who were both claiming the same coat of arms.

Nobody could be more pleased than Richard, his nephew, to see his uncle depart, though later he would realize how badly he needed him to help him deal with the rebellious barons. For his expedition, Richard lent his uncle a thousand marks and sent coffers of gold to both John of Gaunt and Costanza.

Henry's two sisters Philippa and Elizabeth, who accompanied their father, were absolutely dissimilar in character. Philippa was pious, having been brought up very strictly in the Duke of Lancaster's Palace of the Savoy. Her father, with his flair for brilliant marriages, arranged her wedding to John I of Portugal in Portugal. She became the mother of that celebrated Portuguese prince, 'Henry the Navigator', who from his base at Sagres sent out voyages of discovery all over the world. Philippa's marriage was political, to forge a close alliance against Castile. Henry was never to see Philippa again, although they corresponded. Elizabeth on the other hand, was frankly wanton and highly-sexed, but she had been affianced to the Earl of Pembroke when he was scarcely eight. Richard II's half-brother Sir John Holland, a man of a lusty appetite, had made her pregnant, having been banished by Richard for the violent murder of Ralph Stafford in Yorkshire. Elizabeth was now hastily married to John Holland and they both accompanied her father's expedition of seventy-seven ships. Henry's half-sister Catalina, the only daughter of Gaunt by his Spanish wife Costanza, also travelled with her father, and was to make a royal marriage with a Castilian prince.

So Henry was left behind in England, empowered to superintend the important Lancastrian lands and saddled with the administration of the County Palantine while his father was overseas. He was in 1386 aged twenty and his relations with his cousin had worsened because of the honours Richard was bestowing on Robert de Vere and his other favourites. However, between 1382-85 Richard was too generous, giving him the castles of Okehampton, Queenborough and Berkhamstead.

Yet we know too little about de Vere, Earl of Oxford, to form a just estimate of his character. That he was urbane, loved magnificence, and had similar tastes to Richard II, we can readily accept. He had clearly insufficient experience in politics to be a suitable adviser to the King. It was folly and perverse to create his friend Marquis of Dublin around 1385, the first marquisate in English history and later 1st Duke of Ireland, actions certain to antagonize the barons, already opposed to the King. When he was very young - not uncommon in that age - he had married Philippa de Couci, daughter of Isabella, Edward III's eldest daughter, and so Richard's first cousin. Later in 1387 Robert de Vere repudiated his marriage, to enable him to marry his mistress Agnes Lancecrona, one of Richard's queen's ladies. This particularly infuriated the King's youngest uncle, Thomas of Woodstock, recently created Duke of Gloucester, now aged thirty-two.

Gloucester was the leading member of the party opposed to Richard's Court, a tactless, aggressive, difficult man, who almost certainly had designs on his nephew's throne, for he was very ambitious. He had very little in common with his nephew except that they both loved beautiful things. He was one of the five lords who rebelled against Richard II, the so-named 'Lords Appellant' accusing five of the King's counsellors of treason. The other four were Richard Fitzalan, 9th Earl of Arundel, Thomas Beauchamp, 12th Earl of Warwick, Henry Bolingbroke 9th Earl of Derby, who was a moderate at first, only joining the rising later after a meeting at Waltham Cross on November 14th 1387, and Thomas Mowbray, Earl of Nottingham, who now allied himself with the Gloucester faction, though formerly very friendly with the King. His decision was no doubt influenced by his marriage to Arundel's daughter.

The Earl of Arundel, a former governor of Richard II, was of the ancient nobility, a nobleman with distinguished naval and military service, but tactless and quarrelsome and lacking sympathy with King Richard's problems in his youth.

Parliament met during October 1386 - it is known to history as 'the wonderful Parliament', and immediately demanded the removal of the King's Chancellor, Treasurer and friend, Michael de la Pole, recently created Earl of Suffolk, a supporter of John of Gaunt and one of the most efficient administrators produced by the Middle Ages. Loyalty to his friends was one of Richard's best qualities. Although Parliament sentenced Suffolk to be found guilty of peculation and deprived him of his properties and to imprisonment in Windsor Castle, Richard, in a defiant mood, invited him to share in the Christmas festivities. He was, however, compelled to acquiesce to demands for de la Pole's imprisonment when Thomas Arundel, Bishop of Ely, a brother of the Earl's and John Gilbert, Bishop of Hereford, became Chancellor and Treasurer. They were both member of the Gloucester faction.

Angry at their continued interferences, the King refused to attend Parliament and retired to one of his favourite palaces, Eltham. He sent them a defiant message refusing to dismiss even one of his flunkeys at Parliament's command.[14] When Gloucester and Thomas Arundel, a much wiser man than his brother, visited Richard at Eltham, Gloucester hectored his nephew according to Knighton, citing an ancient statute that annual Parliaments must be held. If the King did not attend, Parliament might disperse after forty days' grace.[15] He probably threatened Richard, reminding him of Edward II's deposition. To ensure the King's further degradation, Parliament authorized a commission of fourteen to administer the government, including Gloucester, the Earl of Arundel and his brother, the Bishop of Ely. Even if they were granted these powers for only a limited period, one year, the measure was harmful to Richard's prerogative.

While the young king faced deadly danger in his struggle with the rebellious lords, he thought it politic, together with his beloved Queen Anne, to make a progress in the country, visiting Lincoln, York, Chester and Nottingham Castle. No doubt these visits were designed to give him support in the country and to enhance his popularity. During his visit to Lincoln in March 1387, he gave the mayor John Sutton the privilege of having a sword carried before him.[16] It is almost certain that Richard presented the mayor with a sword either on this occasion or in 1389. It can be seen there, to this day, in Lincoln's historic Stonebow and Guildhall in the heart of the city, a beautiful specimen of an actual 14th century fighting sword with the arms of Edward III engraved on the pommel.

During September 1387, Bolingbroke about to be appointed commander of the Lords Appellant army, heard the joyful news that his young wife Mary de Bohun had given birth to their eldest surviving son, born in the gatehouse of Monmouth Castle in South Wales. Who could have predicted that the infant would be the future Henry V? There is a legend that Bolingbroke, when he crossed the River Wye near Walford, was told the good news by the ferryman, and so delighted was the Earl of Derby that he gave the man all the ferry's dues and tolls.[17]

Robert de Vere, Earl of Oxford, was still in high favour with King Richard, and living in considerable state in Chester, where he had been created Justice of Chester and later Justice of North Wales. When the King summoned Gloucester, Warwick and Arundel to his counsel in early November 1387, they openly defied him, publishing an 'appeal of treason' against the King's friends, de Vere, Archbishop Neville of York, the Earl of Suffolk, and Sir Robert Tresillian, Lord Chief Justice, hated because of his harshness to the rebels after the Peasants' Revolt, and Nicholas Brembre, sometime Mayor of London, and known for his loyalty to the King in the City. The action of the 'Lords Appellant' in ridding themselves of Richard's friends, was illegal and without the sanction of Parliament. To gain time the King referred the 'appeal' to Parliament, allowing time for Neville and Suffolk to escape abroad, while Brembre loyally remained in London seeking support for the King, and Tresillian went into hiding in Westminster. When Henry Earl of Derby and Mowbray Earl of Nottingham openly took sides against him, the King was never to forgive them, but for the present, deprived of his friends, he was powerless.

In the Civil War that ensued, Henry took a leading part, revealing considerable skill as a soldier. He was more than a match for de Vere, outwitting him at the battle of Radcot Bridge in Oxfordshire and routing him with his four thousand men. However, de Vere was no coward. December 20th dawned a bitterly cold, foggy day, when the desperate de Vere deserted by his men escaped across the frozen Thames, with his horse, to seek refuge abroad. Henry's military prowess may have been inherited from his grandfather Henry of Grosmont, first Duke of Lancaster, who was one of his cousin's most brilliant commanders in the earlier Hundred Years' War. Richard, virtually a prisoner in the Tower, and deeply grieved by de Vere's crushing defeat, had only one consolation: the devotion of his Queen Anne.

One contemporary eye witness of these dramatic events was the chronicler Adam of Usk, born in Usk, Monmouthshire about 1352, who relates the triumphant march of the five Lords Appellant through the streets of Oxford. He watched it, engaged in his legal work, "on the way to London from the battlefield where the Earls of Warwick and Derby led the van, the Duke of Gloucester the main body, and the Earls of Arundel and Nottingham the rear."[18]

Arundel, whatever his defects as a man, was an able naval commander, having during the last year beaten the French in the battle of Cadsand (off Margate). A hundred ships laden with wine were captured and distributed free to the people of London, thus gaining their favour. Unfortunately King Richard was suspected of being pro-French by the Londoners.

There he lay in the Tower at the mercy of the rebellious appellants, while they besieged the fortress. An ugly, menacing mob made constant clamour outside its walls. While they fraternized with the private armies of the insurgents, Richard was in a desperate predicament. There is no doubt that his uncle Gloucester wanted to depose him and have himself proclaimed king. Fortunately for the King, two of the appellant lords, Henry of Derby and Mowbray of Nottingham, were strongly opposed to this scheme, for they had joined the other appellants to get rid of Richard's counsellors rather than to destroy him. Richard's presumptive heir to the throne was neither John of Gaunt, now in Spain, Edward III's fourth son, or Gloucester (Edward's youngest son), but Roger Mortimer, Earl of March, descended through the family line from Lionel, Duke of Clarence, Edward's third son.

Confusion reigned everywhere, but two powerful intermediaries, Henry Percy, Earl of Northumberland and Archbishop Courtenay of Canterbury, arranged a parley for the appellant lords with Richard, while their forces blockaded the King. The evidence is somewhat conflicting as to what happened now. The rebel lords reproached him bitterly for his perfidy in allowing some of his friends to escape, but Richard would not have submitted tamely to their demands. It was only when Henry of Derby, secretly gloating at his power, respectfully invited the King to come to a window to show him the menacing besiegers outside that he was compelled to give way.[19] For Richard it was an agonizing decision, since his high notion of his *regalitée* always dominated his mind. Then Gloucester brutally told his nephew:

> "This is not a tenth of the people who want to take our part to destroy and exterminate false traitors to the King and kingdom."[20]

Under protest Richard was compelled to agree to the arrest of his devoted tutor Sir Simon Burley, Sir John Beauchamp and the Justices who had supported the King as to the illegality of some of the Lords Appellant's actions. It seems certain that Richard was actually deposed for two or three days towards the end of December 1387, but the whole affair was hushed up. Evidence exists in the *Whalley Abbey Chronicle*, supported by the Duke of Gloucester's confession in 1397: "I was in place ther it was communed and spoken in manere of deposyl of my liege lord, trewly I knowlech wele that we were assented therto for two dayes or three..."[21] The events of December 1387 may well have given Henry Bolingbroke a taste for power and sharpened his ambition, but he was very intelligent and realized that the time was not ripe for action. In constant touch with his father in Spain, he was well aware that John of Gaunt would never have agreed to Richard's deposition.

The Merciless Parliament,[22] so-named because of its vindictive treatment of the King's friends, who were on trial for treason, assembled in February 1388 in the White Hall. Miss Clarke in her well argued work, *Fourteenth Century Studies*, has stressed the doubtful legality of much of the proceedings. It was at worst, a travesty of justice.

Far from disapproving of this trial, Henry of Derby showed his satisfaction by sending to the other four appellants, lavish gowns, baldekyn of Cyprus gold, to wear during the trials, signifying their unity. Clad in these garments, the Lords Appellant strode into the White Hall of the Palace of Westminster, flaunting their power, but careful to make their obeisances to the King. Richard, who had lately been released from the Tower, sat on his throne, a mere puppet king, while the chancellor, Bishop Thomas Arundel, was on the woolsack. The White Hall was crowded not only with great barons, but with knights and burgesses.

Three of the accused, Robert de Vere, the Earl of Suffolk and Alexander Neville, Archbishop of York, were now exiled abroad and unable to face their trials. To accuse such men of high treason against the King was absurd, because de Vere was manifestly trying to rescue Richard's prerogative and Suffolk had earlier been charged with peculation, and he was clearly not guilty of treason. In the fourteenth century it was not possible to extradite people accused of crimes, for no extradition treaties existed between countries.

To somebody living in the twentieth century it seems manifestly unjust that the accused should be denied the right to see his indictment, or indeed the time to prepare his defence. Richard's friend Sir Nicholas Brembre, who at least had the courage to face his trial, had abused his office of mayor and interfered with the course of justice. However, as he had attempted to raise an army in the city to fight the Lords Appellant, it is hard to understand how he was guilty of treason against the King. Richard made a valiant attempt to save his friend without avail, for he was beheaded for his crimes.

Henry of Derby at least did his utmost to save the life of his cousin's old tutor, Sir Simon Burley. Sensing that he and Mowbray were milder in opposition to him than the others, Richard had asked Henry and Mowbray to dine with him on the night in the Tower when his uncle Thomas of Gloucester had threatened him. Richard had then wrung a promise from them both that they would support Burley. It was all in vain. Richard made desperate attempts to save his life and even Edmund of Langley, Duke of York, a spineless character, fiercely remonstrated with his younger brother Duke of Gloucester, in open parliament, pleading for mercy. Gloucester, vindictive and ruthless, refused to listen. When Anne of Bohemia, although it was deeply humiliating, knelt before Gloucester to plead for Burley's life, he told her sarcastically that it was she, the Queen, and her husband, who needed to pray. To condemn an old, helpless man in weak health for alleged treason of plotting the deaths of the Commission Council in 1386 was shameful. He was highly esteemed by his contemporaries, described by Froissart as "this right noble and courageous knight". A learned man with a fine library, his faults lay in his extravagance and encouraging Richard to have a too high notion of his prerogative. No act of the Merciless Parliament gave greater pain to the King than the execution of Burley, with the exception of Robert de Vere's banishment, condemnation to death in his absence and subsequent death in a boar hunt a few years later.

The bloodiest chastisement was reserved for Sir Robert Tresillian, hated by the people for his cruelty, for which they were probably justified. He was dragged out of sanctuary in Westminster Abbey, and already condemned to death without a semblance of a trial, drawn on a hurdle and hanged on Tyburn Gallows.

The Lords Appellant gained materially from the Merciless Parliament, for they were voted the enormous sum of £20,000. For the most part during the next year, their rule was undistinguished, unimaginative and sometimes oppressive, as in the legislation passed in the Statute of Labourers against the poor. They had no representatives in Parliament to defend their interests. The most notable event was the border warfare between England and Scotland when the immortal Harry Hotspur, eldest son of the first

Percy Earl of Northumberland, lost the Battle of Otterburn (1388) or the Battle of Chevy Chase (though the Earl of Douglas was killed).

Richard now longed for the return of Henry's father, John of Gaunt, as much as he had once yearned to get rid of him. He knew that he was the only man his uncle Gloucester feared. He had learnt much from his bitter humiliation by the Lords Appellant. Henceforward he would walk warily, seeking by slow degree to gain his revenge. Gloucester and his confederates wanted to keep Richard in subjection, but the King, now aged twenty-two, ardently wanted to govern himself and overthrow their rule. His dramatic act in the Council Chamber on May 3rd 1389 of announcing his intention to govern himself, his household and his realm, astonished his opponents by its audacity, but they could do nothing to prevent it.

Six months later, on November 13th, John of Gaunt sailed into Plymouth, to be given a joyous welcome by the people of England, for they considered that he had achieved a brilliant triumph in the marriages of his two daughters. Philippa, Henry Bolingbroke's favourite sister, was now Queen of Portugal, while Catalina, the daughter of his second marriage to Costanza of Castile, was now the wife of Henry, son of John I of Castile.

Meanwhile the Duke of Lancaster had acquired further riches, having by skilful negotiations sold his wife Costanza's claim to the throne of Castile for the immense sum of £100,000, and an annual pension of £6,600. Gaunt now became the King's most trusted counsellor, highly venerated and absolutely faithful to him. On December 10th, together with the Duke of Gloucester and the Earl of Arundel, he was present at a Council at Reading. Richard was astute enough to know that he urgently needed his eldest uncle's conciliatory gifts to make peace between him and the Lords Appellant.

Henry must have been very uneasy during this period and fearful of Richard's attitude towards him, because of his success against his favourite de Vere at Radcot Bridge and his actions during the Merciless Parliament. However, Henry still remained a Councillor and attended a Council on September 13th. It is far from certain what John of Gaunt thought of his son's part against the King. We can only speculate.

19

Derby would have consulted his father when joining the appellants, but it is not known whether John of Gaunt expressed disapproval. The French source, *Chronique de la Traison et Mort de Richard II*, invaluable for its revelations leading up to the King's deposition, betrays anti-Lancastrian bias at times. It is certain that Richard discussed Henry with his father, and the Duke of Lancaster, knowing his nephew's unpredictable nature, might have said "he deserves to die", but it is inconceivable that Gaunt actually pressed the King to execute his son.[23] So far as is known, the Duke of Lancaster's relations with his son were constantly felicitous, and if he made some chance remark as "he deserves to die", he did not intend the King to take it literally.

John Hardyng, Harry Hotspur's loyal esquire, accuses John of Gaunt in his Chronicle of falsely claiming in Parliament that Edmund Crouchback, from whom he was directly descended, was in reality the elder brother of Edward I. Hardyng's Chronicle is biased in favour of the Percys and cannot be relied on.

It is certain, however, that later in 1399 Henry Bolingbroke, desperate to find justification for his own weak claim to the throne, raised the same question, but some learned jurists ruled against him.

John Kirby in his biography of *Henry IV of England* is hardly fair to Henry's cousin when he states: "Richard had already shown himself completely lacking in all those qualities of tact and statesmanship that were required of a king, and it was only the advantage of possession combined with the strength of his subjects' reverence for 'such divinity' as doth hedge a king, which kept him on the throne for another twelve years." However, during the early part of his personal rule, when he had thrown off the hated yoke of the appellants, Richard showed some imaginative ability, and even a gift for statesmanship, particularly in his Irish policy. Richard has been criticized not without reason for his choice of favourites and advisers, but he made one excellent appointment, Edmund de Stafford, Keeper of the Privy Seal, a distinguished scholar and administrator, who became his Chancellor in 1396. He was much esteemed, and Henry IV was to reappoint Edmund de Stafford, Chancellor in 1403. One of Richard's chief faults was his extravagance and too great generosity to his friends. It was indeed foolish of him to quarrel violently with the City and people of London during 1392. So anxious was Richard to gain John of Gaunt's support that he made one of his worst mistakes. The County Palantine of Lancaster and its Dukedom were made the hereditary property of Gaunt and his male heirs in tail. He could not foresee that Henry Bolingbroke, Lancaster's heir, would one day threaten his throne.

Henry, watchful and wary, and mistrustful of his cousin's smiles, wanted some excuse to take him away from Court, and his father would have advised him on this course. In 1390 there was a truce between England and France, but a brave young warrior about Henry's age, named Jean de Boucicaut, with three other French knights, about this time issued a challenge to joust for the honour of France. Since he was one of the best jousters in England, Henry, a young nobleman of twenty-four, was eager to take up the challenge, possibly brought to England by John of Gaunt's Lancaster herald. Others to take part in these jousts held at St. Inglevert, halfway between Boulogne and Calais, were Sir John Holland, King Richard's half-brother, and Henry's brother-in-law, recently created Earl of Huntingdon, Thomas Mowbray, the Earl Marshal, and Harry Hotspur, who had recently been ransomed by Parliament after capture by the Scots at the Battle of Otterburn.

Jean Froissart has described vividly the jousts held at St. Inglevert "at the beginning of the merry month of May", but it is the Monk of St. Denys, also a contemporary chronicler, who relates that Henry and his knights "were recognized as the bravest of all the foreigners". Froissart relates the distinguished part the Earl of Huntingdon played, jousting with relish against the gallant Boucicaut. These medieval jousts required enormous courage, but Huntingdon managed to avoid being wounded, although Boucicaut pierced his shield and slid the point of his lance right over his arm.

At St. Inglevert there seem to have been as many as sixty English knights and esquires, led by John Holland and Thomas Mowbray, while Henry Bolingbroke's party included nine others: his half-brother Thomas Swynford, son of Gaunt's mistress Katherine Swynford, John Beaufort, Henry's illegitimate half-brother, and Henry Percy (Hotspur).

There are in the British Library some beautifully illuminated illustrations of Froissart, including jousts of St. Inglevert, near Calais, in 1390, in which Henry Earl of Derby took a prominent part. The ladies crane forward on the balconies to watch their gallants display their skill. All is light and colour.[24]

It was Jean de Boucicaut, the gallant Marshal of France and a much travelled knight and crusader, who would often discuss with Henry the war then being waged between the Teutonic Knights and the Infidel in the lands bordering the Baltic. Henry, all his life strictly orthodox as a churchman, longed to lead such a crusade. He was also anxious to escape from his cousin's Court, realizing how sorely Richard missed his favourites and how much he grieved for them. In his decision to travel extensively he was influenced by his father, John Duke of Lancaster. Gaunt was eager to remove Henry from Court, well aware that his nephew Richard, brooding on the tragic fate of his favourites, would all too often be reminded of them by the presence of his son at Court.

Such travel by a medieval nobleman of royal blood was not only costly, but required enormous organization. Indeed it is doubtful if Henry could have undertaken his two journeys without his father's financial assistance. John of Gaunt advanced £4,000 out of the vast riches he had brought back from Spain after selling his claim to the throne of Castile.

Among his many activities Henry's grandfather, Henry of Grosmont, first Duke of Lancaster, had been a crusader and Bolingbroke may well have wished to follow his example. Over forty years before, Henry of Grosmont had made a pilgrimage to Prussia.

By 1390, Henry, now aged twenty-four, was the father of three sons: Henry of Monmouth, Thomas (later the Duke of Clarence), and John of Lancaster. His loyal friends throughout his life were his household officers and knights, who had served the House of Lancaster for many years; squires such as Thomas Erpingham, John Norbury, one of his most intimate friends, Hugh Waterton his Chamberlain, Peter Bukton, Thomas Rempston, his half-brother Thomas Swynford, a member of his party at the jousts at St. Inglevert, and William Willoughby, son and heir of Lord Willoughby. All these men accompanied Henry's expedition, but the total number sailing from England was at least seventy, including six minstrels, twenty-five grooms and many servants.

Before embarking on his first journey, Bolingbroke went to see his wife Mary de Bohun and his father and family at Hertford Castle to say farewell. Together with Mary he then made offerings in Lincoln Cathedral. For the sea voyage to Prussia where Henry planned to go, large stores of provisions had to be prepared. Live cattle and horses were taken on board a ship at Boston in Lincolnshire. The next two years were among the most important in his life and were to enhance and add lustre to his name and stature.

II   Travels and Pilgrimages

The most useful work relating to the travels of Henry Earl of Derby is *The Expeditions to Prussia and the Holy Land made by Henry Earl of Derby (afterwards King Henry IV) in the years 1390-1 and 1392-3*.[1] This account is taken from the rich store of records of the Duchy of Lancaster preserved at the Public Record Office.

Derby was more fortunate than his uncle Duke of Gloucester, who was commissioned by Richard II during September 1391, probably in an attempt to get rid of him, to press ships and sailors at Orwell in Suffolk to take him and his company to Prussia to negotiate with the Grand Master. According to Walsingham, Gloucester set out on this expedition against the wishes of the people of England, who feared King Richard's tyranny. Owing to violent storms, the ships bearing the King's uncle touched on the Danish, Norwegian and Scottish coasts, but were compelled to return to Tynemouth. Gloucester finally reached his house at Pleshey in Essex, relieved that he was not a victim of the tempests.

It was on August 8th 1390 that the ships carrying Henry Earl of Derby and his entourage to Prussia sailed into the German Ocean, Copenhagen and a large portion of the Baltic. At Leba on the Pomeranean coast, Derby sent three of his trusty companions, Robert Waterton (brother of the invaluable Hugh), Thomas Tolty and John Payne as an advance party. Henry himself with some of his company landed at Rixholt, where they had a meal of bread, beer, mead and fish, while the rest went on by sea to Danzig. The Earl of Derby then travelled in a cart as far as Putzig, where he bought a horse and saddle and spent the night of August 9th in a mill[2] - a strangely humble lodging for the cousin of the King. Meanwhile a Lancaster herald took horse with letters from John of Gaunt to the Grand Master at Marienburg.

The Teutonic Knights had been founded in the twelfth century to succour sick and wounded Christian soldiers in Palestine and to wage war against enemies of the faith. By the middle of the fourteenth century they had become an aggressive, territorial power on the Baltic, using violence to convert unbelievers.[3] Feigning religion, they murdered men and women and forced their children to submit to being baptized.

The transport of vast supplies for Henry's army through densely forested marshy country was a gigantic undertaking. Necessarily much of the organization depended on Henry's invaluable Chamberlain, Hugh Waterton.

According to the accounts kept by the Earl of Derby's treasurer, flat-bottomed boats known as 'Prames' were used for the transport of the heavy baggage, but at Königsberg a large number of baggage-carts, driven by Prussian carters, were hired, taking some of the baggage to Wisterburg Castle. A great prince in medieval times was expected to travel in style, and at the start of the expedition from Boston, sheep and cattle, chests of hangings and tapestries needed for Henry's hall and bedchamber, his armour and many other items had been loaded on to the ships. So, the army wended its cumbrous way to the Lithuanian border. On August 21st the expedition reached *The Wyldrenesse*, now called the Grauder Forest, lying between Insterberg and Raguit. Wild frontier passes separate Prussia from Lithuania.

Henry received a warm welcome from Marshal Rabe, the Commander of the Teutonic Knights. By August 24th they were crossing the Memel river. What delighted Henry was to be received by the Master of Livonia's musicians, who played some rousing airs.

He acquitted himself well in the battle fought on August 28th, clearly impressing Marshal Rabe. This was much to his credit, for Derby's military experience was limited in 1390 to the Battle of Radcot Bridge, three years earlier, when he had routed Robert de Vere.

Now he played a valiant part in besieging Vilna, the strongly fortified capital of Lithuania and important for its trade. Among Henry of Derby's troops, according to the chronicler Walsingham, were many skilled bowmen, one of whom was the first to reach the top of the rampart and plant his banner. Fierce fighting ensued and terrible slaughter. Whilst crossing a ford, one of

Henry's young knights, Sir John Loudeham[4] was badly injured and he was taken to Königsberg (now part of Russian territory) where he died on August 28th. Despite the use of mines and engineers, the defence of the two forts was so effective that the besiegers were compelled, owing to sickness and lack of powder, to withdraw after five weeks.

When he returned to Königsberg, Derby took with him a number of Lithuanian children, but he behaved kindly to them, clothing, feeding and boarding them at his own expense. According to Walsingham, eight Lithuanians were made prisoners, while one 'Henry' Lettowe, named after Derby, was eventually taken to England. His treatment of these children shows him to have a tender side to his character.

Derby spent nearly four months, including Christmas and the New Year (1391) at Königsberg. It was a gay and pleasurable time, filled with hunting parties, jousts, tournaments and hawking. As Henry was a keen musician, he delighted in the minstrels and fiddlers who were in continual attendance on him, enlivening the long Prussian winter. Dressed in his favourite red and black gowns and clad in furs against the cold, Henry enjoyed himself enormously.[5] Whilst at Königsberg, he received many presents, such as horses and hawks, deer, three young bears, a wild bull and perhaps an elk.

We know that Henry interceded for two of his knights who had been taken prisoner, and that Derby herald was sent with letters to Jagiello, King of Poland in November. For this purpose Henry (according to correspondence between Henry and Conrad von Wallenrod on February 22nd 1391) asked an eminent Pole in Marienburg to intercede on their behalf with the King, but he was unsuccessful. While he still sojourned at Königsberg, Henry heard that his wife Mary de Bohun had given birth to his fourth and youngest son, Humphrey, who was to play such a prominent political rôle during the reign of Henry's grandson, Henry VI.

At Danzig, Henry stayed about six weeks, having to take lodgings for his large entourage in two places. One for himself and various people in a house in Danzig that belonged to a burgess named Klaus Gottesknecht and the other for a larger portion of his retinue, a little out of the city in the mansion of the Bishop of

Leslau or Cujevic. Henry of Derby whilst staying in Danzig, would often make 'pilgrimages', visiting and making offerings at four churches daily.

It is known that at least sixty people were still on his payroll, including Sir Peter Bukton, the Steward, Hugh Waterton, the Chamberlain, Robert Waterton, the Marshal, Richard Kingeston, the Treasurer, Hugh Herle, the Chaplain, John Derby, the herald, Thomas Erpingham, John Norbury and Thomas Swynford. Six permanent minstrels also attended Henry.[6]

He now planned to return to England and two ships under the command of Prussian masters, but with English pilots from Boston, were chartered. On his journey home carpenters were employed to provide cabins for Henry's party, stables for the animals and cages for the hawks he was taking with him. The ships were also laden with every kind of store, baggage and provision for food and drink. About March 31st 1391 Henry Bolingbroke embarked with his entourage, and the voyage home, described as long and tedious, took a full month. Except for occasionally playing at dice, we do not know how Henry occupied the time, but we know that he was fond of chess and had taken his chessboard to Prussia, so it is probable he sometimes played this game. Henry and his men disembarked at Hull at the end of April, but some of the baggage was ferried across by coasting vessels to Boston. Then it was taken across Lincolnshire to Bolingbroke. From his birthplace Henry made a pilgrimage to Bridlington Priory in Yorkshire.

His reputation for bravery was greatly enhanced after his crusade to Prussia, and he now became very popular with the people. It is unlikely that King Richard would have welcomed his cousin with much enthusiasm when he returned home. Uneasily he could sense that Henry was a power in the land, and he would watch him ever more warily.

At court Henry indulged in lavish expenditure, buying a gilded barge in which eight boatmen in red cloth and scarlet hood were employed in rowing him on the River Thames. When he rode on land, a herald would precede him, wearing his coat of arms of red leopards and gold fleur-de-lis with a blue label.[7] We do not hear of any mistresses, and Henry seemed happy in his home life, with Mary de Bohun, visiting her in her favourite manor of

Peterborough. Unlike his father or his sister Elizabeth, he was curiously chaste by nature. It is possible that Bolingbroke, after his wife's early death in 1394, had a bastard son called Edmund Labourde, alleged to have been born in 1401 (when he was King). He died in infancy.[8]

During the November Parliament, Henry was a trier of petitions, but for a nobleman, ambitious and able, he was clearly not given important enough work to satisfy his tremendous energy. True, he was a member of his father's party, given the diplomatic task of converting the truce between England and France into a lasting peace. In seeking such a peace, King Richard revealed that he had the makings of a statesman, but his policy was violently opposed by the war party at home headed by the Duke of Gloucester who hankered for a renewal of the war with France, nostalgic for the glorious victories of Edward III and the Black Prince.

Henry's father John of Gaunt, was eager to meet Charles VI, King of France, and his embassy was very impressive. It included not only Henry, Earl of Derby, but Richard's half-brother the Earl of Huntingdon, Edmund of Langley, Duke of York, and Sir Thomas Percy, younger brother of the Earl of Northumberland and later Earl of Worcester, probably the most able of the Percys. The French had omitted nothing to honour their English guests. The English embassy were escorted by as many as a thousand horsemen.

After they landed at Calais, the Count of St. Pol accompanied them from Calais to Amiens, where it was proposed they negotiate the peace. A magnificent banquet was given in the Archbishop's palace for members of John of Gaunt's embassy, where they were entertained by Charles VI of France, and John of Gaunt sat on the King's right side. For the occasion the King of France wore a purple gown sewn with jewels and pearls. The English were lodged at Malmaison, but little progress was made in the negotiations. The French requested that the English surrender Calais and raze its fortifications, while the English demanded the unpaid balance of King Jean II's ransom and the *status quo* of the Treaty of Brittany.

But the chief question in dispute was Aquitaine. Since 1152, the year of the marriage of Eleanor of Aquitaine with King Henry

II, the sovereignty of the duchy had been owned by England, but the French claimed it as part of their country. Richard, however, ever willing to please his uncle John of Gaunt, proposed to relinquish the sovereignty of the duchy and confer it instead on a new dynasty, the Duke of Lancaster and his heirs. It was an imaginative, statesman-like proposal, but full of hidden danger. In retrospect, it would have been more politic if Richard had considered more carefully the possibility of a hostile Duke of Lancaster in the future.

For Henry, however, it offered glittering prospects. Not only would he own, on the death of his father, the Lancastrian lands and palatinate in England, but the rich land of Aquitaine overseas, held by the King of France. Nobody at this stage foresaw the obstacles preventing this dream being realized.

By the summer of 1392 Henry was again planning a further expedition to Prussia. He still had the ardent resolve to join the frequent campaigns of the Teutonic Knights, being very much a man of action. On June 22nd, the King's letters of protection were granted to Henry of Derby and his companions, Hugh and Robert Waterton, since they were about to go abroad, and on February 6th 1392 Derby's letter was renewed, to last a year. He was then described as "tarrying abroad".

John Capgrave the chronicler suggests that Henry of Derby's reasons for travelling overseas were to avoid political troubles at home. 1392 was a critical year for King Richard, for he again engaged in a violent and rash quarrel with the city of London: unwise because it cost him their lasting enmity, for they had eventually to pay him £10,000 for their pardon and £3,000 for their continuance. Richard indulged in every sort of extravagance and his civilized court was very expensive to maintain.

Just before Henry left for abroad, Mary de Bohun, Henry's wife, gave birth to an infant daughter, christened in Peterborough Cathedral and named Blanche, after Blanche of Lancaster, Henry's mother.

He could not have embarked on his second voyage to Prussia if his father John, Duke of Lancaster, had not on July 1st granted him 2000 marks a year, to be paid quarterly out of the receipts arising from his possessions at Tatbury and Bolingbroke. Gaunt later added a gift of 1000 marks for his son's voyage to Prussia.

Finally Henry sailed on July 24th from Heacham on the Wash, together with about two hundred men in three ships, fully laden. A great part of his provisions had been bought at Lynn. The voyage seems to have been faster than the one in 1390, for the ships arrived on August 10th at Putzig and Danzig, where Henry stayed a fortnight, probably in the house of Gottesknecht, his host of two years before.

When he reached Königsberg on September 2nd, Henry was given the disappointing news that the Teutonic Knights no longer required his services. The reason for this cool welcome is by no means clear. It may be that there was not at this time any campaign in which he could serve. A German authority, Professor Prutz, opines that disputes as to the right of bearing the banner of St. George was the cause of the contention. St. George was both the patron of Englishmen, especially since the founding of the Order of the Garter in 1348, and St. George was also the chief patron saint of the Teutonic Order. In their own territory the Teutonic Knights insisted they should have precedence, with the sole right among other contingents to bear St. George's banner. It is possible conflicting views prevailed on this matter. Richard Kingeston, Archdeacon of Hereford, was again Henry's treasurer for war, having been released from his ecclesiastical duties. His accounts record that the Teutonic Order paid him £400 towards his massive charges undertaken on their behalf.[9]

Henry now decided that some of the party must return home as they were no longer needed. Towards the end of September, the Master of the Ship *Ludkyn Drankinaistre*, received 100 marks or £66.13.4d for his hire, taking home Robert Waterton and his brother John, four esquires, about six minstrels, twenty-six valets of the house and others, including William Pomfreit, the Clerk of the Kitchen, an important official. Henry of Derby's main party still remained very strong, about fifty altogether, including seven officers and knights, ten squires, two heralds, the trumpeter and a hired guide. Leaving Danzig on September 22nd, Derby arrived at Schonec the same day, where he halted two or three days. There he was joined by Sir Thomas Erpingham. By October 4th he had arrived at Frankfurt-on-Oden.

Entering Bohemia, then part of the Roman Empire, at Gorlitz three days later, he reached Prague on October 13th. There he stayed at the court of King Wenceslas, brother of his cousin Richard's Queen Anne, for eleven days. The reign of Wenceslas was somewhat disorderly for he tolerated the Hussites, followers of John Hus, the religious reformer, and was later deposed in 1400. For three days Henry was the King's guest at a favourite country house named Bedeler. On October 21st and October 22nd, he paid devotional visits to the ancient castle of Hradschin in Prague and offered prayers at the relics in the castle at Karlstein.

Whilst in Prague, Henry of Derby made many purchases, including goldsmiths' ware and two super-altars for his chapel. Scutcheons of Henry's heraldic arms were also bought and Lancaster herald was busily employed painting these arms in his room in Prague and later in Vienna. Whenever their lord made an extended stay, it was customary for the heralds to hang in his hall the insignia of his rank.

By November 4th Henry had reached Vienna and crossed the Danube. Here he was the guest of Albert of Hapsburgh, Duke of Austria, who was most helpful. Knowing that Henry had an ardent desire to visit Palestine, he used his good offices to write to the Senate of Venice requesting them to supply a galley to transport Henry to Jaffa and back. For this purpose Henry commissioned his steward Sir Peter Bukton and others, including Mowbray herald, to travel with 14 horses to Venice, to provision the galley for the voyage. A bargain was struck at 2,785 ducats for the return journey. During his short stay in Vienna, Henry amiable by nature, became friendly with Wenceslas's younger brother Sigismund, King of Hungary, who three years later was to lead a calamitous European crusade against the Turkish invasion of Hungary.

Henry's longing to visit Jerusalem increased as the means of doing so was aided so benevolently by the powerful and influential princes he had encountered. His journey through parts of Austria, Styria and Carinthia was leisurely, but through the rugged country of Friuli in Italy the roads were narrow and treacherous and the wheels of Henry's carriage were broken, so that he had to exchange it for two others.

When Derby entered Venice on November 30th, the Signory treated him with high honour, giving him a public reception after voting 300 ducats. For about three weeks Henry stayed at a house on the Isola di San Giorgio, facing the palace of the Doge, while his men made many purchases for the voyage in the surrounding countryside. The winter was hard that year (1392) and nine men were continually employed to break the ice between Venice and Portogruaro, where boats had to be hired to carry baggage. It is recorded that Henry gave oblations on December 2nd at St. Mark's and, according to Capgrave, he was entertained by the Doge. They made oblations together and Henry on his own at various Venetian churches.

For the ordinary pilgrim wishing to visit Jerusalem during the medieval age, the voyage was a fearsome ordeal, for the ships were filthy and overcrowded, and Turkish pirates were always a menace. For Henry the voyage could be undertaken in considerable comfort. He sailed from Venice about December 22nd or 23rd, giving oblations on Christmas Day at Zara on the Dalmatian coast; then on by Lisea, Corfu and Modon, at the south of Morea. He stopped for a short stay at Rhodes, inhabited by the Knights of St. John since 1300. Here fresh supplies were procured and some necessary repairs to the rudder were made, while he made a courtesy call on the Grand Master Heredia in his palace. Then they continued their journey to Jaffa, where fish were bought and an ass hired to carry food to Ramla.

We do not know for certain how many of Henry's entourage accompanied him to Jerusalem, but they included Sir Peter Bukton, the Steward, Kingeston, the Treasurer, a guide Antonio, Mowbray herald, and perhaps Chelmeswyke a squire, and a few valets.

The pilgrimage of thirty miles from Jaffa to Jerusalem was probably made on foot, since there is hardly a mention of a mule or horse here. Derby's pilgrimage was very brief, but it was to make an enormous impression on his mind for the rest of his life. At Jerusalem, wax candles were bought and Henry made offerings of six ducats at the Holy Sepulchre and the Mount of Olives. About eleven years later, after Henry had usurped his cousin Richard's throne, we find him writing to the Emperor of Abyssinia at the beginning of his reign telling him of his ardent desire to visit the Holy Land and to rescue the Holy Sepulchre from the hands of the Infidels.[10] Perhaps the emotion was all the more powerful in Henry that he was suffering remorse for his crime. Wylie, an important authority on Henry IV, relates an adventurous journey by the Earl of Warwick during 1393 to Jerusalem, but he was only ten days between landing at Jaffa and re-embarking.

After Henry returned to Jaffa, fresh food was bought there and he sailed straight to Famagusta in Cyprus, where he stayed in the castle. During his brief sojourn there, he sent three members of his party as ambassadors to James I of Lusiquan, King of Cyprus. Everywhere he went Henry was received with honour, and it is probable that the King of Cyprus presented him with a leopard. On the island of Rhodes repairs were made to Henry's galley, and a cabin made for the leopard.[11] By this time the Earl of Derby had received further gifts from his hosts of falcons and a parrot. He also had in his entourage a converted Turk, whom he brought back from Rhodes and baptized by the name of Henry. He later travelled with Henry's confessor Herle to Peterborough in Northamptonshire.

At Venice on his return journey, Derby stayed about three weeks until April 10th (1393), spending Easter there and having eight more escutcheons hung at St. Mark's, as memorials of his visit. Again Henry stayed on the Isola di San Giorgio. The Signory behaved generously, awarding him 100 more ducats, "So that he could go back to his own country well pleased with us". He moved on to Treviso, where he stayed until April 26th, while Kingeston remained behind in Venice to settle accounts. Chests had to be found for all the fine things Derby had purchased in Venice: collars of silver and a collar and chain of gold. Whilst in Treviso, Henry stayed in the friars' convent and hectic preparations were made to transport his baggage. Finally on April 28th the main party left Treviso, the falcons borne on horseback for Vicenza, and the luggage in carts for Padua. Mowbray herald went in advance of his lord to announce his arrival in Milan about May 12th or May 13th.

According to Capgrave, Henry was entertained by Gian Galeazzo Visconti, Seigneur of Milan, nicknamed the Count of Virtues[12] and created Duke of Milan three years later. Gian Galeazzo was a friendly, urbane Italian nobleman, a contrast to his brother Bernabo, who was a lustful tyrant. Henry only stayed a few days in Milan, but a gradual friendship ripened between them, so that they would correspond for many years. Gian Galeazzo showed Derby the tomb of his own uncle Lionel of Antwerp, Duke of Clarence, who had died in Milan, after his brief marriage to Violante, Gian Galeazzo's sister. Other tombs he showed his guest were those of St. Augustine and Boethius. Henry also showed some diplomatic skill in arbitrating in a dispute between Visconti and a house of Austin Friars.

At twenty-six Henry was very attractive to the fair sex and whilst in Milan he completely won the heart of Gian Galeazzo's young cousin Lucia Visconti, a girl of fifteen. Lucia, passionate by nature, was so smitten with the English prince that she vowed she would wait until the end of her life to marry Henry of Derby, even if she was to die three days later. When her family wanted her to marry a German prince, Frederick of Thurugia, she refused to do so.[13] She subsequently married Edmund Holland, Earl of Kent at Milan (1406), but her life was mostly unhappy. We do not know what Henry's sentiments were for this young girl, but he must have been flattered by Lucia's passion. However, he was always faithful to Mary de Bohun while she lived.

Whilst in Milan, Derby bought some velvet for which the city was renowned, some of it cloth composed of velvet and gold. About May 17th Henry left Milan and passing through Vercelli and Chivasso, arrived in Turin four days later, where he gave alms at St. Anthony's.[14] When travelling through France, parts of Burgundy and Champagne, he did not pass through Dijon, its capital, where Philip the Bold (Le Hardi) ruled, possibly because Philip was away at the time.

In Paris he spent only two nights, and there Charles VI's two uncles, the Dukes of Berri and Burgundy, acted as his guide. On June 28th he travelled to Calais and from there crossed to Dover. Four boats were needed to carry the men and the baggage, including the leopard, ashore.

From Dover, Henry of Derby went by the old road through Canterbury, breakfasting at Sittingbourne on July 1st. He reached Rochester with his leopard on July 2nd, whence he travelled to Dartford on the 3rd and was in London by July 5th. Aged twenty-seven, he had gained in stature and was now a prince of European renown, exchanging letters with Sigismund King of Hungary and Gian Galeazzo Visconti, Duke of Milan. To the 'Count of Virtue' Henry sent presents of greyhounds, horses and three large silver gilt hunting horns, and Galeazzo sent his new friend gold and red Milanese velvet.

Prominent poets such as John Gower showered Henry of Derby with praise, eager to get his patronage. Disliking Richard II's personal rule, Gower about this time deserted the King for Henry, sending him a slightly grovelling letter in which he declared his allegiance. He wrote:

> I send unto myn owne Lord,
> Which of Lancastre is Henry named.

The poet presented him with a new edition of *The Confessio Amantis*. Bolingbroke also knew Geoffrey Chaucer quite well, presenting him in 1395 with a scarlet gown lined with 101 civet skins costing £8.8s.4d.

There would have been joyful reunions with his wife Mary de Bohun, now the mother of five children and living mostly in Peterborough. Bolingbroke Castle was mostly used to store all the massive records of the Duchy of Lancaster and a room in one of the towers was the audit room. A manuscript of the seventeenth century describes it.[15]

"The Castle of Bolingbroke was built by William de Romaray Earle of Lincolne and ennobled by the birth of King Henry 4th who from thence took his name. The towne standes in a bottome and ye castell in the lowest part of it, compassed about with a large moat fed by springs...It hath 4 strong forts or ramparts wherein are many rooms and lodgings...The entrance into it is very stately over a faire draw-bridge." By the seventeenth century, however, it had gone much to ruin and decay.

The castle even had its ghost. "It was reputed to be haunted by a certaine spirit in the likenesse of a hare, which at the meeting of ye auditors doeth usually cume between their legs and sometymes overthrows them and soe passes away..."[16]

Henry, a soldier of some ability, was certainly influenced by the prevailing superstition of the medieval fourteenth and early fifteenth century.

III   The Deposition

One of Richard II's worst mistakes was to have alienated the citizens of London, for they were never really to forgive him. It was Queen Anne, his beloved spouse, who interceded on behalf of the City of London. She addressed her husband in extravagant words. "My King, my husband, my light, my life! Sweet love, without whose life mine would be but death." Though the letters patent restored the city's liberties, they did so only conditionally "until the King should otherwise ordain".

When Richard and Anne kept Christmas at Eltham, the citizens requested mummers to entertain them. Richard had lost his early popularity, and his policy to seek a lasting peace with France was very unpopular. His cousin Henry Bolingbroke was much more their idea of a popular hero. We find Henry Bolingbroke spending Christmas 1393 with his father John of Gaunt at Hertford Castle, probably his favourite home, and in the New Year he was one of the challengers in the jousts and tournaments. Charles VI of France sent his own jester to amuse Henry of Bolingbroke during the festive season. After Bolingbroke had left for London in January, he showed his affection for his wife Mary by sending her at Hertford a present of oysters, mussels and sprats.

During January 1394, Parliament opened in the White Hall of Westminster Palace; Richard II was present, clad in splendid robes with the bishops to the right and the barons to the left. It was notable for a strong attack by the Earl of Arundel on John of Gaunt, for Arundel was very jealous of the King's elder uncle. Henry was present at this parliament and no doubt resented Arundel's accusations. Arundel was also opposed to the peace policy with France advocated by Gaunt and considered that the grant of the Duchy of Aquitaine was derogatory to the King. He complained that the Duke of Lancaster had been seen walking arm-in-arm with Richard and that the King was wearing the collar of the

Lancastrian livery. Furthermore, Gaunt had squandered public money on a private war against Castile. Richard answered Arundel's accusation. If he was seen arm-in-arm with the Duke of Lancaster, he claimed it had no significance, for he did the same with his other uncles. As to Aquitaine, it had been fully sanctioned in Parliament. Arundel, a fiery nobleman, had also complained of the lack of facility of being able to speak without fear, but that charge was brushed aside. The accusation of squandering money on the Spanish war was dismissed on the grounds that its cost had been freely voted by Parliament. A portion of it had been acknowledged as a personal debt by Gaunt, but Parliament had agreed to remit it because of his services to the crown. Arundel was forced to make a public apology, and retired from the Council breathing resentment against the King and the Duke of Lancaster.

On April 30th, however, the King granted his enemy a special pardon for all his past misdeeds, a point raised by Arundel, when he was accused of treason a few years later.

The year 1394 was one of royal deaths. Probably on March 24th, there died Costanza, the Duke of Lancaster's Spanish-born second wife. For many years this had been a marriage of political convenience, though during the 1380s Gaunt had relied on her judgement in Iberian affairs. Wronged by her husband because of his continuing liaison with Katherine Swynford, mother of four of his children, Gaunt suffered little by her decease. Nevertheless he honoured her more in her death than in her life. He travelled to Leicester for his wife's magnificent burial in Newark College, for which he spent the enormous sum of £550. The monk of St. Denys is incorrect when he says that Costanza's tomb was so magnificent in St. Paul's.[1] He should have referred to the tomb of Henry's mother, the Duchess Blanche. Now there would open the possibility of legitimizing Gaunt's four Beaufort children by Katherine Swynford.

At the beginning of July, there died at the tender age of twenty-four Mary de Bohun, Henry's wife. She died in childbirth, having just given birth to her younger daughter Philippa, a future Queen of Denmark. It is likely that Henry was keenly distressed, but he lacked his cousin's emotional nature and his natural reserve made it more difficult for him to express his feelings. She was given a splendid funeral in the College of Newark, Leicester, and twenty-four poor men were provided with gowns of black cloth. Henry also donated a hundred marks to the dean and canons of the church to provide for repairs and new buildings.[2] He was not to marry again until after he usurped his cousin's throne.

A month before, on June 7th, Richard's queen was suddenly taken ill with the plague while staying at Sheen and died the same day. Anne of Bohemia was much loved. The King's grief was intemperate, and typical of the monarch. He ordered that the palace of Sheen where he had passed such happy hours with her, should be razed to the ground, including the moated manor and the island sanctuary of La Noyt with all its memories. The chronicler Adam of Usk calls her "*Illa benignissima domina*" and so she was, for her influence on her husband was always on the side of moderation. If anybody could curb Richard's sudden unbridled rages, it was Anne. Bereft of so many of his friends, by execution or by exile, he had become more and more dependent on his beloved queen.

After his friend Robert de Vere had been killed in a boar hunt during 1392, whilst exiled in Louvain, Richard had arranged that his body should be brought back and reburied in the de Vere family vault at Earls Colne in Essex, a magnificent ceremony not attended by Derby, Arundel, Warwick and Gloucester.

Anne was given a majestic funeral. Her body first lay in State in St. Paul's, to be carried in a procession to the burial service in Westminster Abbey on August 3rd.[3] Unfortunately the proceedings were marred by the Earl of Arundel's rudeness and lack of courtesy in not attending the funeral procession and then arriving late at the main ceremony. Richard was so incensed that he seized a wand from a verger and struck Arundel so heavily that he fell bleeding to the ground. Richard may be criticized for giving way to his violent temper in such a sacred place, but Arundel must also be blamed for showing his spite. After being arrested he was released after a week.

If Anne had lived, she would surely have saved Richard from his worst excesses and misjudgements. And if she had given birth to a prince, it is difficult to conceive how Henry of Bolingbroke could have usurped his cousin's throne.

He did not accompany King Richard to Ireland during the autumn of 1394 in his successful attempt to pacify the people, to revitalize English rule and subdue Gaelic and Anglo-Irish lords by a skilful blend of firmness and conciliation. This expensive expedition to Ireland was the first by an English king since 1210[4] (King John's reign) and is an example of King Richard's imaginative statesmanship. Henry stayed at home, a member of the Council responsible for ruling England while the King was overseas. Meanwhile Richard was obliged to return to England before he had completed his mission, because the Lollards, who had many influential supporters in high places, were causing trouble at home.

What was Lollardy? It was a movement for ecclesiastical reform initiated by the teachings of John Wycliffe, the great religious reformer, who had died in 1384. It advocated clerical poverty and the translation of the Bible into English, while condemning transubstantiation, the sacraments and celibacy for the clergy.

Many members of Richard's court were attracted to Lollardy, including Sir Richard Stury, Sir Lewis Clifford, and Sir John Montagne, third Earl of Salisbury, the King's loyal friend. Both Henry Bolingbroke and his cousin were devoutly orthodox. Richard II in a fit of temper might have threatened Sir Richard Stury with "the foulest death that may be" if he ever broke the oath of recantation, but the most heinous act of Parliament ever to pass into the statute book occurred during the early reign of Henry IV, the *De Heretico Comburendo* (1401) which committed heretics to be burned to death.

Overall, the winter of 1394-95 was an unfavourable period for Henry of Derby, for his hopes were finally shattered that he would inherit the rich lands of Aquitaine from his father. The Gascons were opposed to the grant of Aquitaine to the Duke of Lancaster, arguing that it was not consistent with their special relationship with the English crown. This argument was accepted by a Council meeting in England, much to the chagrin and disappointment of Gaunt and Bolingbroke. For the time being Henry's ambitions were frustrated.

Another factor was to cause Henry a great deal of uneasiness, even unhappiness. To the surprise and consternation of many,

Henry's father married his mistress Katherine Swynford in Lincoln Cathedral in February 1396, for the purpose of enabling their three sons and one daughter to be legitimized. Almost a year later, in January 1397, Henry's half-brothers and half-sister of the Beaufort family were declared legitimate in Parliament, a proceeding apparently approved of by Pope Boniface IX, who previously had issued a bull confirming the Duke of Lancaster's marriage to his mistress and confirming that in future their children, John, Henry, Thomas and Joan Beaufort, would be regarded as legitimate. According to Froissart it was owing to John of Gaunt's fondness and pride in his children by Katherine, which determined his action. For Henry, however, although his relations with his half-brothers were satisfactory, it was a heavy blow. He firmly resolved after he usurped his cousin Richard's throne to ensure by an addition to the Act that none of the Beauforts could ever inherit the throne. Up until this time, it would have seemed to the ambitious, wary Henry that he would have had a good chance of succeeding eventually to Richard's throne.

Two high-born ladies, Henry's sister-in-law, Eleanor de Bohun, Duchess of Gloucester and Philippa Hastings, Countess of Arundel, in particular disapproved of John of Gaunt's third marriage, resenting that his wife was now entitled to precedence on all State occasions.

However, Henry's chances further receded when Richard began negotiations for his marriage to his child-bride Isabelle, eldest daughter of Charles VI of France. During March 1396, Richard's new favourite, his first cousin Edward, Earl of Rutland (heir of Edmund of Langley) and Mowbray, Earl of Nottingham, now high in Richard's favour, negotiated successfully in Paris a truce with France for twenty-eight years, whereby King Richard would marry Princess Isabelle, a child of not yet eight years. Rutland was an able negotiator, a clever linguist, who was to translate into English *Le Livre de la Chasse*, written by Gaunt's friend the Count of Foix.[5] In proposing to marry Isabelle, the King was clearly prepared to wait until his bride was of a riper age to give him children.

It was by no means clear that Roger Mortimer, Earl of March, descended through his mother Philippa from the female line of

Lionel of Clarence (Edward's third son) was Richard's heir. It is interesting to note that the King proposed to Charles VI in June a possible marriage between Henry of Bolingbroke's eldest son (the future Henry V) and Michelle, Charles's youngest daughter, but nothing came of it.

It has seldom been remarked that one point in favour of Richard's marriage to a French bride was an attempt to end the great schism, the crisis caused by the appointment of two rival popes at Rome and Avignon,[6] and unresolved until the Council of Constance (1414-17). During the marriage negotiations, Richard and Charles planned to abandon both the Roman and the Avignon popes, so that a Council of the church could choose their own candidate as pope.[6] However, this plan never materialized.

Richard's marriage to Isabelle of France was violently opposed by his uncle Thomas of Gloucester and by the Earl of Arundel, both members of the war party. It was also very unpopular in the country. Among those who accompanied King Richard to France on his third visit were Henry of Bolingbroke, and the King's three uncles, the Dukes of Lancaster, York and Gloucester. The presence of the new Duchess of Lancaster, though welcome both at the French and English courts, caused embarrassment to the Duchess of Gloucester and other ladies. The ceremonies were extremely lavish. Henry was clad like the other lords in a long red velvet gown, decorated with Anne of Bohemia's heraldic white bend. In the British Library among the Harleian manuscripts there is a vivid scene of Richard greeting his French bride outside the royal tent. At twenty-nine, Richard had an intuitive understanding of the mentality of a little girl, and with an adroit blend of flattery and make-belief, fascinated the Princess. For Henry it was an ominous sign that the pair seemed so well suited. Although the English lords such as Mowbray and Rutland gave her lavish presents, Henry merely gave her a gold greyhound, one of his own badges, adorned with a ruby and a large pearl hanging from its neck.[7]

The Brut Chronicle tells how Isabelle was borne to St. Nicholas's church (now no more) in Calais, to be "worthily weddyd with the most solemnite...and all mynystries of Holy Churche".[8] Isabelle made her state entry into London on November 23rd and was crowned Queen of England in Westminster Abbey on January 7th 1397. There were ominous murmurings among the people at this most costly marriage, the expenses amounting to about £200,000.

According to Froissart there was tension about now between Henry of Bolingbroke and his father, because in his eagerness to leave Richard's court, Henry was keen to join his kinsmen, the Counts of Hainault and Ostrevant, in an expedition against the rebels in Friesland. Gaunt was anxious for Henry's safety. He had many conversations with the Duke of Guelders, who was visiting England, and became so worried when Guelders described the hazards of campaigning in Friesland that he forbade him to go. He asked the King to add his prohibition.

Meanwhile the King's uncle, the Duke of Gloucester, was openly hostile to Richard's policy towards France and matters came to a head when in April 1397, the King restored the fortress of Brest to the Duke of Brittany. Richard was absolutely entitled to do this, for Brest had been pledged to England while the war lasted for a loan of £20,000 and the grant of Castle Rising in Norfolk. Now there was a twenty-eight year truce.

The *Chronique de la Traison et Mort de Richard Deux d'Engleterre*[9] begins the history of Richard's downfall at this point. At a feast held in Westminster, the King was taking wine, hypocras and comfits (sugar-plums) as was the custom, when Gloucester insolently remarked among other things: "Sire, you ought first to hazard your life in capturing a city from your enemies by feat of arms or by force, before you think of giving up or selling any city which your ancestors the Kings of England have gained or conquered." He could have said nothing more calculated to incense Richard. Henceforward Gloucester was a marked man.

His activities were now those of a traitor, conspiring together with the Abbot of St. Albans and the Prior of Westminster. He also sent a sealed letter to Henry Bolingbroke, Earl of Derby, requesting him to come to a meeting at Arundel, and to others of the Lords Appellant of 1389, to the Earl Marshal Mowbray, Earl of Nottingham, to the Earl of Warwick and to Thomas Fitzalan Arundel, Archbishop of Canterbury, brother of the Earl of Arundel. While Derby, Nottingham, Thomas Fitzalan and Gloucester were dining together at Arundel Castle during July 1397, guests of the Earl of

Arundel, Warwick arrived, to be told by Gloucester, "My brave man, you must take the same oath as we have taken." Warwick, who was inclined to be cowardly, asked: "My Lord, what do you wish me to swear?" Gloucester answered, "You will swear as we have done, if you please, to be true and faithful to the realm, and also to be true and faithful to each other." That night the Lords rested at Arundel Castle and on the morrow heard mass. So far the account in the *Chronique de la Traison* is so vivid and convincing that one can believe in its veracity. Now according to the author of the chronicle, the conspirators withdrew to a council chamber and "there were of accord to seize the noble King Richard, the Duke of Lancaster and the Duke of York, and that they should be put in prison for ever; and that all the other lords of the Council of King Richard should be drawn and hung." This plan was to be put in execution during August. It seems incredible that Henry of Derby would agree that his own father should be imprisoned in perpetuity, for so far as is known they had always been on the best of terms. There is every reason to doubt this part of the story, although the rest surely tallies. Ten years before, the same conspirators had met at Waltham Cross for the appealing of treason the Archbishop of York, the Duke of Ireland (Robert de Vere), the Earl of Suffolk, Robert Tresillian and Sir Nicholas Brembre.

The name of the author of the *Chronique de la Traison* is not known, but it is thought to be a French Benedictine monk, who resided near Windsor. Although biased in favour of Richard II, it is by no means untrustworthy, although in parts unreliable.

One reason for the conspiracy at Arundel was to forestall the vengeance of Richard, who had never forgiven the Lords Appellant for depriving him of his friends and executing them. It was betrayed to King Richard by Mowbray, Earl of Nottingham. Richard heard the news of the conspiracy while he was dining with his half-brother the Earl of Huntingdon and other members of the Council, at his beautiful London home in All-Hallows,[10] on the banks of the Thames. Richard acted immediately, riding to Pleshey in Essex, the home of his uncle the Duke of Gloucester, escorted by a large body of archers and men-of-arms. Gloucester was persuaded to accompany the King to London, where he was arrested on the way, handed over to Richard's friend Mowbray,

Earl of Nottingham, to be taken by ship to Calais and mysteriously murdered, smothered in a feather bed, as was alleged. As Gloucester was in frail health, the rigours of his confinement might have caused his death, but it is more likely that Richard was responsible. Gloucester's death was carefully concealed. He was popular with the Londoners, but the King's most venomous enemy, constantly involved in treasonable plots against him. Meanwhile the Earls of Rutland and Kent had arrested the Earl of Arundel, one of the leading appellants, and also the Earl of Warwick. Both were lodged in the Tower.

Clearly there were vital reasons for concealing the extent of the conspiracy. Richard had surely been apprised that his cousin Henry had been present with the other conspirators at Arundel. Perhaps he would have liked to impeach Gloucester, but he dared not, fearing that if he were to do so, his uncles the Dukes of Lancaster and York would not condemn their brother, the Duke of Gloucester. What Gaunt thought of his nephew the King's arrest of his brother Gloucester, we do not know. His strong sense of royal authority conflicted with his fraternal sentiments and he certainly did not approve of Gloucester's attacks on Richard. Gaunt would have been aware of the dangers confronting his own son Henry as a political supporter of Thomas of Woodstock,[11] Duke of Gloucester, in 1387-1388. He was only too aware of Bolingbroke's vulnerability.

Henry himself feared arrest. News was received from Calais that Gloucester was dead, from natural causes it was said officially, but another story told of his murder. Making a giant effort to feign unconcern, Henry gave a splendid banquet in his Fleet Street mansion. The menu consisted of all sorts of exotic dishes, thirteen curlews, thirteen doves and thirteen parrot, all elaborately designed by the King's painter, John Prince.[12] He had his State barge freshly covered with forty ells (yards) of canvas in the regal red and white.

The Parliament that was about to assemble on December 17th 1397 was one of the most dramatic of those troubled times. Richard was protected by his private bodyguard of 400 Cheshire archers, striking awe into the hearts of bystanders, for their reputation was very bad, addicted as they were to unruly behaviour and even violence. Henry arrived at the Westminster Parliament attended by a large armed retinue. He was careful to say that they were all completely at the King's service.

Richard, determined on his revenge, followed the same procedure as the Merciless Parliament, appointing eight new Lords Appellant, the Earls of Nottingham (Mowbray), who had turned King's evidence, Kent, Huntingdon, Somerset (Beaufort), Sir Thomas Despenser and Lord William Scrope. These were to appeal Gloucester, Arundel and Warwick of treason. Before Gloucester died in his Calais prison, Sir William Rickhill, one of the King's justices, had been sent to obtain Gloucester's confession, and he returned with a general confession of treason, though containing no details of the recent plot at Arundel.

The Earl of Arundel was the most courageous of the accused, refusing to beg the King's mercy when confronted by his enemies the Duke of Lancaster, Henry of Derby and the King's friend, Sir John Bushy. Adam of Usk, whose Lancastrian sympathies strongly favoured the Earl of Arundel, dramatically described the proceedings. The Duke of Lancaster presided as High Steward, and bitter accusations were flung by Gaunt against Arundel. He accused Arundel of treason. "'I am no traitor,' responded Arundel. 'If no traitor, why had he earlier asked for a special pardon,' demanded Gaunt. 'To close the mouths of my enemies of whom thou art one,' was the spirited retort."

When Bushy referred to the faithful Commons, Arundel answered vehemently, "Where are those faithful Commons? The faithful Commons are not here. They, I know, are sore grieved for me, and I know that thou has ever been false." There was a certain grandeur about the man, despite his grave faults. Bolingbroke's attack on his old colleague and former Lord Appellant, hardly shows him in a favourable light, though he had never forgiven the accused nobleman of calling his father a traitor. "Didst thou not say to me at Huntingdon (in 1387) where first we gathered to revolt, that it would be better first to seize the King?" Arundel replied: "Thou, Earl of Derby, thou liest at they peril! Never had I a thought concerning our Lord the King save what was to his welfare and honour." After being sentenced to death, he was executed the same day on Tower Hill, brought to execution by his own son-in-law, Thomas of Mowbray, Earl of Nottingham.

Thomas Arundel, Archbishop of Canterbury, at least had the courage to try to save his brother. He argued with some skill that the special pardon granted to the Earl in 1394 should not have been repealed. However, the Archbishop was impeached and denounced as a traitor by Parliament. It would have been better if Arundel had been allowed to be tried. It is not clear whether the Archbishop had been guilty of treason, but he had been of Gloucester's party and supported him during the Merciless Parliament. If he had been present at the proceedings at Arundel, it was hardly the loyal conduct expected of an Archbishop of Canterbury. Arundel and King Richard certainly disliked one another, and by banishing him overseas Arundel became a bitter and dangerous enemy. According to the Rolls of Parliament (in the reign of Henry IV), Richard promised to recall Arundel, but faithlessly broke his word, despite swearing by oath on the Cross of St. Thomas of Canterbury. Arundel was to draw much closer and become more intimate with Henry of Bolingbroke after he was later exiled and Henry was to depend largely on this able man after his usurpation of the throne. Arundel is alleged to have remarked to Mowbray of Nottingham, after he had been created Duke of Norfolk, that he was not the first Primate to be banished and that he suspected Norfolk and other lords would also be exiled before long.[13] A prediction which proved true.

When Mowbray, the Earl Marshal, was ordered as Captain of Calais to produce the Duke of Gloucester for trial, he could not because he had died mysteriously at Calais. He was sentenced after death, but his prior confession was clearly an admission of treason. His grovelling pleading to Richard for mercy is nauseating, for he richly deserved to die. Neither Henry nor Gaunt seem to have protested when Gloucester was declared posthumously a traitor. Henry's father made no attempt to preserve his younger brother's life. He was fifteen years older than Gloucester. Nor did he insist that the mysterious circumstances of Gloucester's death should be investigated, though Henry, who enjoyed good relations with his uncle during the 1390s, set up an inquiry after his usurpation. Perhaps Gaunt knew too, how treacherously his brother had behaved towards the King or again he may have kept silent, fearing for his son Bolingbroke. He was not criticized by his contemporaries, but posterity has been puzzled ever since.

When Thomas Beauchamp, Earl of Warwick, now an old man, was tried, he behaved "like a wretched old woman, he made confession of all...wailing and weeping and whining", according to Adam of Usk. A complete contrast to the fortitude of the Earl of Arundel, though Warwick had never been very prominent during the Merciless Parliament.

When Richard examined him, he had admitted that the Duke of Gloucester, the Abbot of St. Albans and a prior recluse of Westminster had influenced his treason. The King then replied with his favourite oath, "By St. John the Baptist, Thomas of Warwick, your confession is more pleasing to me than the value of all the lands of the Duke of Gloucester and the Earl of Arundel." Warwick was condemned to exile, to be guarded by Sir William Scrope in the Isle of Man and his possessions forfeited. He was later transferred to the Tower of London, until liberated by Henry IV.

Henry was now in favour, for he was created Duke of Hereford; Edward, Earl of Rutland, son of Edmund, Duke of York and Isabella of Castile, became Duke of Aumerle; Mowbray of Nottingham was created Duke of Norfolk, the Earl of Kent was made Duke of Surrey, the King's half-brother the Earl of Huntingdon, always loyal to Richard, was created Duke of Exeter. Sir William Scrope became Earl of the Isle of Man, the Lord Despenser, Richard's friend, Earl of Gloucester and Sir Thomas Percy became Earl of Worcester. According to the *Chronique de la Traison*, King Richard held a great court and gave a magnificent feast where the heralds received costly gifts from the lords and ladies and My Lady of Exeter, Bolingbroke's sister (the wife of the newly created Duke of Exeter), was awarded the prize as the best dancer and singer.

During December 1397 there occurred the celebrated quarrel between Henry and Thomas Mowbray. Unfortunately we have only Henry, the newly created Duke of Hereford's story, uncorroborated by anybody else. Apparently they met accidentally while riding from Brentford to London in late December 1397. "We are about to be undone," exclaimed Mowbray, now Duke of Norfolk. When Henry asked why, Norfolk replied fearfully, "because of Radcot Bridge", where Henry had defeated Robert de Vere. Hereford then remarked that they had been pardoned for that offence. Norfolk, however, insisted that Richard had never forgiven them and would give them the same treatment as he had dealt with the others. He told a wild story, according to Hereford, saying that the world was a marvellous one and a false, that there was a plot to kill Henry and his father at Windsor after the Parliament, and that four lords, who were intimate with the King, Exeter, Surrey, William Scrope, Earl of Wiltshire and the Earl of Salisbury, were involved in the plot.

There was no obvious need for Henry to make Norfolk's story public, but he repeated what had happened to his father, who advised him to take it to the King. There is evidence that relations between Mowbray and John of Gaunt, Duke of Lancaster, were very bad. Adam of Usk related in his chronicle before the Parliament held at Shrewsbury "that Mowbray laid snares of death against the Duke of Lancaster as he came thither, which thing raised heavy storms of trouble." But the Duke, forewarned by others escaped the snare.

According to the *Chronique de la Traison*, Richard was about to set out for Shrewsbury when Henry presented a petition to him, accusing the Duke of Norfolk of treason, and challenging him to battle as a disloyal traitor to the realm of England. Henry after removing his black bonnet, accused Thomas of Mowbray "as a traitor, false and recreant towards your royal majesty, to your crown, to the nobles, and to all the people of your realm." When the King asked Norfolk, "What have you to say, Thomas?" the Duke answered that Henry of Lancaster was a false traitor and disloyal subject. Later Henry made further charges against Mowbray at a Court of Chivalry at Windsor, suggesting that as Captain of Calais, he had embezzled several thousand pounds trusted to him for the payment of the garrison. His second serious accusation was that Norfolk was involved in the murder of "his dear uncle", Thomas of Woodstock, Duke of Gloucester. Richard had been formerly fond enough of Norfolk, a useful courtier, but he now turned against him.

As for Henry, the King mistrusted him, all the more because he had recently been warned against him. *The Brut Chronicle*[14] has a curious story that "a worshipful clerke that was an astronomer at his court had warned Richard that he shulde be slayne and destroyed be a toode (toad). So he told him to beware of toads, for a toode shulde destroye hym, and then the King thoute and mervayled in his mynde how that shulde be. At a royal feast at Christmas many lords came in their gayest robes, among them Henry Earl of Derby in a gowne broydered al aboute with toadys...and ever aftyr he had this Henry, Erle of Derby, ym Ielway and mytrust, supposing that yt shulde be he that shulde destroy hym..." Surely Richard saw this quarrel of Hereford and Norfolk as an ideal opportunity to get rid of both, to destroy them. Yet despite Froissart's criticism, the King did make some attempt to reconcile them. The chronicler suggests, "We shulde rather when he herde the wordes fyrste have sayde to them bothe, 'Ye are two lordes of my blode and lygnage wherefore I commaunde you bothe to be in peace and lette nouther hate nor rancour engendre (breed) bytwene you, but be frendes, lovers and cosyns togyther..."

Shakespeare with his sure instinct for drama, begins his great play *The Tragedy of King Richard the Second* with Henry Boling-broke's appeal for treason, but his character is hardly developed in this play. Only in *Henry the Fourth*, Part I, does he cast full light on the weary, disillusioned man and King, haunted by conscience, who had seized Richard's throne.

According to Froissart, the Duke of Hereford found no difficulty in getting his father, his uncles the Dukes of York, Aumerle and Surrey to go bail for him, but the Duke of Norfolk found nobody for this purpose and after being arrested was taken to Windsor where master armourers from Germany were employed to make his armour. As for Henry, he applied to his friend the Duke Gian Galeazzo of Milan, a correspondent since his pilgrimage to the Holy Land. Only too happy to help, Galeazzo sent him four Milanese armourers, skilled in adjusting the intricate pieces of steel and leather.

The trial by battle was scheduled to take place on Monday, September 16th 1398 at Gosforth Field just outside the prosperous cloth town of Coventry. The day before, Henry, who was staying at Kenilworth Castle, went to take leave of the King, while at break of day the following morning Mowbray did the same, visiting the Carthusian Monastery to hear three masses,[15] afterwards riding to his tent to have his armour put on by his esquire, Jacques Felm of Bohemia.

Loving pageantry as he did, Richard attended in great state, accompanied by all the nobility of England, by the new Archbishop of Canterbury Walden, and the Count of St. Pol, a gallant French nobleman whom, it was said, had been entrusted with a mission by Charles VI, to request the King Richard not to allow the trial by battle to take place. It was a duel to the death and many suspected that Richard favoured Mowbray rather than his cousin Henry. According to the *Chronique de la Traison*, there were 20,000 archers to protect the King and many men-at-arms.

What happened has so often been described that it is as well to be brief. The contestants were preparing themselves on horseback for the charge when King Richard, with a dramatic gesture, suddenly exclaimed, "Ho! Ho!" a signal that the Trial by Battle should not take place. At the same time he cast down his warden into the list.

One can imagine the amazement on the faces of the spectators, the muttering of many that they had been cheated of their contest, the relief of others mingled with the suspense on that dramatic day fraught with tragic consequences.

After an interval of almost two hours, Sir John Bushy pronounced the King's sentence. He began by praising the bravery of both knights, but "because the matters were so weighty between the two lords" it was decreed by the King that Henry should be banished for ten years, and if he return to the country before the ten years are passed, he shall be hung and beheaded. There were storms of protest, angry shouts because Henry was popular among the people and many thought him innocent. Then the herald in a loud voice to drown the protests read the King's judgement regarding the Duke of Norfolk. His sentence was a very harsh one, exile for life "and shall choose whether he would dwell in Prussia, in Bohemia, or in Hungary" or given the choice to go to the lands of the Saracens or unbelievers. It would seem that Mowbray had been guilty of misappropriating funds while in Calais, for all his lands would be surrendered into the King's hands to reimburse him for the money misapplied for the payment of the garrison.

Norfolk, a ruined nobleman, was never to return. He was allowed ten thousand nobles a year for his own needs and given a pass to travel through Germany so that he could make a pilgrimage to Jerusalem. From there he returned to Venice, where he died of the plague September 22nd 1399, and there at Venice gave his body to that pleasant country's earth,[16] as the Bishop of Carlyle relates.

Both Dukes were made to swear solemn oaths that they would not meet while abroad, or to live in the same country. Henry also swore that he would not engage in any correspondence with Thomas Arundel, the exiled Archbishop of Canterbury, a vow which he later broke. It is fair to add, however, that Richard also broke his promise later that Henry should inherit the vast estates of his father, the Duke of Lancaster.

It was owing to John of Gaunt's intercession with the King that his son's exile was reduced from ten years to six. There is no evidence, however, that the Duke of Lancaster protested against his son's banishment. Indeed he may have thought it partly justified. Nevertheless it was a bitter blow, for aged almost sixty and in failing health, he could hardly expect to see him again. According to Froissart, Bolingbroke wished to visit Hainault, where his kinsman the Count of Ostrevant held sway, but he was persuaded by his father to go instead to Paris and make his court to Charles VI and the Valois princes. For the last two years of Richard II's reign, Froissart cannot be relied on.

Gaunt took leave of Henry at the palace of Eltham when his son said his farewell to the King. A doleful party no doubt, for they were never to see each other again.

> Four lagging winters, and four wanton springs
> End in a word: such is the breath of Kings.[17]

However, Bolingbroke was to return to his native country long before "four lagging winters".

According to Froissart - and there he is almost certainly accurate - when Henry Bolingbroke, Duke of Hereford, departed from London, "there were in the stretes, no thanne forty thousde men, wepyng and crying after hym, that it pytie to here, and soe said: O gentyl erle of Derby, shall we thus leave? This realme shall never be in joye tyll ye retourn again..., and of so noble blode, that none ought to be compared to you..."[18] Such an emotional scene may well have tempted Henry with dark thoughts to usurp his cousin's throne, knowing that Richard was deeply unpopular with the people cheering him on his way.[18] It was about October 13th 1398 that Henry left London, the mayor and leading citizens escorting him to Dartford, and from there to France.

He was at first given a very hospitable reception, and Charles VI allowed him to use the Hôtel Clisson.

While certain acts of Richard II can fairly be described as tyrannical, there was no conscious attempt to institute a *system* of tyranny. If only Queen Anne could have lived a few more years to restrain him from his worst follies. His arbitrary act of confiscation of property against the most powerful of his barons has rightly been condemned, for on October 8th 1398 letters of attorney had been issued on behalf of Henry Bolingbroke, Duke of Hereford, providing power for his attorneys to receive his heritage in the event of his father's death. John of Gaunt was now considered an old man by medieval standards and his health frail. Richard has been also accused of instituting forced loans when he was financially embarrassed, of offering crooked pardons, black charters, of the so-called hated *le pleasaunce*, the buying back of the pleasure of the King by enormous fines. For the fist six years of his personal rule, Richard had revealed a real gift for kingship, but his rash over-confidence in the last two years of his reign were to lead to his downfall. A tragedy for the country because this most civilized, urbane king with his love of art, might have established the renaissance in England long before its flowering in the Tudor age. Much has been written about the King as a tyrant, but the acts of the Lords Appellant in 1387-88 smacked far more of tyranny. Yet to justify Henry's seizure of his cousin's throne is very difficult.

In Paris negotiations were begun for Henry's marriage to Mary, daughter of the Duke of Berri, uncle of Charles VI, but the Earl of Salisbury and the Bishop of Carlyle, both Richard's friends, soon arrived in Paris, charged with securing a dowry for Isabelle, Richard's queen. Salisbury immediately denounced Henry to the King of France, declaring that he was "a traitor who wolde betray his natural soverayne lorde". Henry ever afterwards would never forgive Salisbury, treating him as an enemy when opportunity gave him the power. The negotiations for Henry's second

52

marriage lapsed, and the nobility became very cool. In Paris, Henry, restless by nature, thought of embarking on a crusade with Marshal Boucicaut, his jousting adversary of 1390. Before going he wisely sent one of his knights home to ask his father's advice.[19] The knight reported back to Henry that his physicians diagnosed that John of Gaunt had such a dangerous disease he could not live for long. Bolingbroke at once abandoned any plans to travel, though the Duke of Lancaster did suggest that Henry might visit his sister, Philippa of Lancaster, Queen of Portugal, or his half-sister Catalina, Queen of Castile.[20] However, Henry decided to remain in France.

Then on February 3rd 1399 after a final illness, John of Gaunt expired in Leicester Castle. His magnificent speech in Shakespeare's *Tragedy of King Richard the Second* admonishing his nephew, has no historical truth, although it is recorded in two chronicles that the King visited his uncle on his deathbed. About twenty years later Andrew Wyntoun, prior of Loch Leven (Fife) mentions: The King spoke to him

> rycht curtasly,
> And gaive hym consale
> of dysporte
> Wyth plesand wordis of
> comforte.

Thomas Gascoigne's story of a royal visit, *Loci e Libro Veritatum* (written in 1449), has rightly been treated with scepticism, particularly by Armitage-Smith, Gaunt's able biographer. According to Gascoigne, John of Gaunt, a great womaniser, showed Richard II how his genitals and other parts of his body had putrefied because of constant carnal intercourse with women.

If the Duke of Lancaster feared with some justification that Richard intended to withhold the Lancastrian inheritance from Henry Bolingbroke, he certainly showed fondness for his nephew in his Will, bequeathing him valuable objects, such as his best gold cup, given him by his second wife the Duchess Costanza, his best jewel and a gold dish engraved with the garter motif. He was given a magnificent funeral in St. Paul's, to lie near Henry's mother, the Duchess Blanche, as he desired. It is likely that Gaunt was '*graviter desolatus*' by his son's exile, but the latter part of his life had been spent in propping up Richard's throne. To suggest that Gaunt would have approved of his son Henry's usurpation of Richard's throne is inconceivable. No doubt Henry was sincerely devoted to his father and had wisely deferred to him. In Paris, Bolingbroke and his entourage went into mourning.

Richard's act of depriving his cousin of his rightful inheritance, his worst political mistake, was no sudden whim. Clearly the King had broken his earlier oath and now resorted to a kind of chicanery. Richard was aware that an autonomous palatinate, with the power of the duchy of Lancaster, presented a grave political danger, so after much thought he resurrected the Parliamentary Committee of 1398, which had been created to deal with the Hereford-Norfolk dispute. The Committee now found ingenious reasons whereby Henry Bolingbroke could be deprived of the grant of powers of attorney enabling him to inherit the immense Lancastrian lands. It was maintained that the grant had been made 'inadvertently' and that the Lancastrian inheritance was now forfeited to the Crown, for the Dukes of Hereford and Norfolk were in effect traitors, who could not inherit. The only legal way for Henry to be judged a traitor would have been a trial in open court. On March 18th 1399 the Parliamentary Committee announced that Henry's sentence of six years was changed to eternal banishment, and that all the mighty possessions of the house of Lancaster were forfeited to the Crown.[21]

Little wonder that Henry Bolingbroke was deeply mortified by Richard's unjust action. No owner of any estate, large or small, felt secure any more. All the Lancastrian estates and castles were in the King's hands, to be granted to the royal favourites. Richard was desperate for money at this period to finance a further expedition to Ireland, for Roger Mortimer, Earl of March, recognized as heir presumptive to the throne, Richard's lieutenant there, had been killed in an ambush on July 20th 1390, leaving a seven-year old son Edmund. The King did not want to have to resort to Parliament for further supplies of money.

According to Wylie, whose four volumes on *The Reign of Henry IV* contain invaluable and almost too much detailed material, Henry was known as sweet, courteous, gracious, neighbourly and well-liked during the half year he spent in exile in Paris. It says too little about his duplicity and cunning.

After travelling to Rome in 1397 the deposed Archbishop Arundel had an interview with Pope Boniface IX and managed to persuade him to write to King Richard to ask whether he could be reinstated as Archbishop of Canterbury. Richard indignantly replied that Arundel was a traitor and expressed surprise that the Pope should interfere. At forty-six Arundel was a prelate of considerable experience, both as a churchman and in affairs of State. He had served for some years as Chancellor, eight years as Archbishop of York, and one year as Archbishop of Canterbury. He was extremely able, ambitious and a master of intrigue. During his exile in Cologne, Arundel had brooded on his fall from power, devising means whereby he could recover it. Clearly there was no possibility of being restored to the primacy while Richard held effective power.

Froissart's story that the deprived Archbishop came from London with an invitation from the Londoners to Henry to deliver them from Richard's tyranny is untrue, though there is a possibility that he managed to return secretly to England to take counsel with Bolingbroke's friends and then take their offer of the Crown back to Henry in Paris. According to Froissart, Arundel, disguised as a pilgrim monk, travelled from Valenciennes to Paris, together with a guide familiar with the road. He was soon joined by his young nephew Thomas, bitterly resentful because of his father the Earl's execution, who had succeeded in escaping from the harsh custody of John Holland, Duke of Exeter, Richard's half-brother and Henry's brother-in-law.

Henry and the churchmen plotted in the Hôtel Clisson.[22] Withdrawing to a window the better to think, Henry and the Archbishop discussed the best means of bringing about Richard's downfall. Bolingbroke's ambition would lend itself to enticing thoughts. Might he now occupy Richard's throne. He knew that the King's subjects were deeply dissatisfied with his misrule and that his government was very unpopular.

Henry laid his plans carefully. Whilst in Paris he corresponded with some of the most important people in the kingdom, with Richard's favourite the treacherous Duke of Aumerle, his half-brother John Beaufort, Marquis of Dorset, Henry Percy, the Earl of Northumberland and others. On June 17th 1399 Bolingbroke made a treaty of friendship with Louis, Duke of Orléans, Charles VI's younger brother, then well disposed towards him, later a vindictive enemy. Since 1392 Charles had suffered periodical fits of insanity, and Orléans had been his Chief Counsellor, engaging in a bitter struggle for power with Philip *Le Hardi*, Duke of Burgundy. Henry's treaty with Orléans is supposed to have been witnessed by his three intimate friends, John Norbury, Thomas Erpingham and Thomas Rempston.[23]

After taking leave of the King of France, Henry left Paris for Nantes, where another good friend, the Duke of Brittany, was prepared to help him. It seems likely that he met here for the first time the Duchess Joanna, whom he was to marry as his queen three years later. Pretending that he intended to visit his half-sister Catalina in Spain, Henry with his large escort rode to the royal Abbey of St. Denis, France's Westminster Abbey, where French kings were entombed. Henry's object in visiting St. Denis was certainly to obtain the Abbot's blessing for his proposed invasion of England,[24] an undertaking ostensibly prepared to recover his inheritance of which he had been wrongly deprived. However it was more likely that Henry's secret ambition was to wear his cousin Richard's crown.

According to Froissart, Henry sailed from Vannes with all his followers, accompanied by three vessels manned with men-at-arms and crossbowmen. In reality his force consisted of three hundred men, according to Adam of Usk, a ridiculous number of men to undertake a serious invasion of England. However, good fortune attended Henry from the beginning of the enterprise. It was also very clever and cunning of Henry to conceal his real intention from the English government, and instead of landing in some southern part of Sussex, land at Ravenspur north of the Humber in Yorkshire. Nearby were many Lancastrian castles and Bolingbroke was well aware that he could count on the support of his family retainers. The probable date of his landing was July 4th.[25]

Richard II has been criticized for his incredible folly in departing on his second expedition to Ireland and landing at

Waterford on May 29th 1399. However, there were valid and urgent reasons for avenging the death of Roger Mortimer at the Battle of Kells some ten months before. It was certainly a gross misjudgement on the King's part and rash over-confidence to leave his kingdom at such a time, thus leaving England to the mercy of his cousin who burned with resentment at his maltreatment. It is evident that Henry was much better informed about affairs in England than Richard was of matters in France. He could not conceive that his exiled cousin could even command enough support to invade his kingdom.

Perhaps Richard imagined that by taking Bolingbroke's eldest son Henry (the future King Henry V) to Ireland as hostage, and also young Henry Beaufort, Bishop of Lincoln, and the young son of the murdered Duke of Gloucester, it would deter Bolingbroke from any such attempt. In appointing his uncle Duke of York as Regent while he was absent from the kingdom, Richard had little choice, but it was unfortunate that Edmund of Langley was not a stronger character. Another miscalculation of the King's was to take so many of his friends to Ireland: his half-brother John Holland, Duke of Exeter, the Earl of Salisbury, Sir John Stanley and Bishop Merke of Carlisle, leaving England to the mercy of his fierce critics and increasing enemies.

Prince Henry's curious fondness for the King can be explained by Richard's intuitive understanding of the mind of a boy. Richard was very kind to the eldest son, aged twelve, of his enemy Bolingbroke, at court and in Ireland. Dubbing him a knight, Richard said: "My fair young cousin, henceforth be gallant and bold, for unless you conquer you will have little name for valour." However, having made a long truce with France, he would hardly have approved of Henry's subsequent war with France after he became King. According to the chronicler Otterbourne, after Richard received news that Bolingbroke had landed in England, he said to his cousin, "Henry, my boy, see what thy father hath done to me." Henry and Humphrey of Gloucester (son of Thomas of Woodstock) were confined in Trim Castle when the King left for England.

Meanwhile, while Richard was engaged on his campaign in Ireland, so vividly described by his admirer Créton, the French squire and chronicler, Henry was consolidating his position, moving from Pickering to Knaresborough and from there to Pontefract. When he landed, Henry Bolingbroke was accompanied by the ex-Archbishop Arundel, Thomas Arundel (son of the executed Earl), Sir Thomas Erpingham, Sir Thomas Rempston, John Norbury, and other faithful retainers. Among his most loyal supporters were the Lincolnshire lords, William Willoughby, Roos and Darcy, who immediately joined his cause.[26] Henry cunningly asserted that his reason for returning was to claim his rightful inheritance, and he showed considerable ability and a real gift for publicity in letting a fisherman go round Ravenspur, crying that the Duke of Lancaster had returned for this purpose.[27]

At Doncaster, Henry swore a solemn oath to the Earl of Northumberland that he had only come to claim his inheritance and that King Richard should reign until his death. This is according to Hardyng, who was certainly prejudiced in favour of his patron, Henry Percy (Hotspur). It has been questioned whether Bolingbroke ever swore this oath, but the evidence would indicate its truth. Henry was immensely strengthened by the support and adherence of the Earls of Northumberland and Westmoreland, and their vast number of retainers. At Pontefract he wrote many letters to citizens, prelates and lords "falsely railing, by different artful fabrications, against the King Richard and his government." He falsely maintained that Richard was plotting the sale of Guienne and Gascony for private gain. No subterfuge or distortion of the truth was too great, so long as they served his purpose in overthrowing the King. At Pontefract he even asserted that Edmund Crouchback, from whom he was directly descended, the younger son of Henry III, was in reality the older brother of Edward I, and had been put aside because of his deformities. If there was any truth in this old story - and it was subsequently disproved by jurists - he would be the rightful king, not Richard.

It was no accident, no whim of fortune or fate that made Henry seize his cousin's throne. There are some pregnant lines in Act III, part 2 of Shakespeare's magnificent play *Henry IV* when he says:

> God knows that I had no such intent,
> But that necessity so bow'd the State
> That I and greatness were compelled to kiss.

Bolingbroke was no reluctant usurper. It is just untrue that *necessity* (England's plight under Richard's misrule), together with his despairing haste to yield power, virtually thrust the Crown into Bolingbroke's hands. The evidence would show that Henry, a crafty dissembler, carefully made his plans to seize his cousin's throne. So, to accuse Henry of fatalism is false, for he exulted in displacing Richard. Ambition and a lust for power should be stressed, rather than fatalism.

The poet Daniel, whose work[28] greatly influenced Shakespeare, especially regarding his view of Henry's culpability, stresses Richard's misrule and the almost inevitable trend of events that caused his downfall.

Henry mustered a large army at Doncaster. It was a masterly stroke to advance to the west, where between Bristol and Berkeley only Despenser, Bishop of Norwich, Richard's loyal friend, Sir William Elmham and a few others made any attempt to resist Henry's forces. The governor of Bristol Castle, Sir Peter Courtenay who sympathized with Henry's cause, surrendered the castle, and three of Richard's Ministers, Bushy, Scrope and Green, who had taken refuge there, were executed without trial and their heads sent in a white basket to London. To the citizens of London Henry wrote that he had come over to claim his rightful inheritance. "I beg of you to let me know if you will be on my side, or not, and I care not which, for I have people enough to fight all the world for one day, thank God".[29]

After making a show of resistance, the Regent Duke of York tamely submitted to Henry, who welcomed his desertion with the words, "Good uncle, you are right welcome and all your people." Among those at Bristol in the train of Thomas Arundel (the ex-Archbishop) and Henry Bolingbroke was Adam of Usk, the celebrated chronicler, who relates[30] that Henry had threatened to pillage Usk, Adam's native birthplace and the surrounding country, but he managed to dissuade him. It was known that Alianore, the daughter of Richard II's half-brother the Earl of Kent, intended to make some show of resistance. Adam also used his influence with Henry and Arundel at Ludlow to achieve the release of Thomas Prestbury, Abbot of Shrewsbury, who was three years later to attempt to mediate between Henry IV and Hotspur before the Battle of Shrewsbury. Adam's chronicle is of considerable value and interest because it is the work of an independent individual and not that of a monastic compiler, reflecting the politics of his House with its shifting sympathies. All the same, Adam is sometimes biased in favour of Lancaster.

On Henry's landing, the Regent York had immediately sent Sir William Bagot to Ireland to apprise King Richard. He arrived on July 10th, but the King delayed too long his return, influenced, it is said, by his treacherous favourite, the Duke of Aumerle, who intended to betray him. According to the *Traison*, Richard was very angry and much agitated, exclaiming that his good uncle of Lancaster had told him truly that he had done wrong to pardon Henry so often, "and yet he offends again". Richard sent the loyal Earl of Salisbury to rally the loyalists of Cheshire, while the Council favoured a return to Waterford and embarkation for South Wales. It was not until July 25th that the King eventually reached Milford Haven in South Wales, to be told the terrible news of the fall of Bristol, the desertion of his Regent York, the execution of his friends Bushy, Green and Scrope, and that his triumphant cousin Henry of Lancaster now commanded a large army. What was worse, he was informed by the Earl of Salisbury that his army had deserted him, and that his friend Aumerle and Thomas Percy, Earl of Worcester, steward of his household and younger brother of the Earl of Northumberland, had also forsaken him. Leaving South Wales in the first days of August, he reached Conway Castle in North Wales, one of the strongest of his fortresses, by the 12th. Richard's movements were reported to Henry, for he was well served by his spies.

Meanwhile Bolingbroke had been very active, moving from Gloucester, Ross, Hereford, Leominster, Ludlow and Shrewsbury and thence to Chester. He had advanced 160 miles in ten days,[31] arriving there on August 9th. At Conway Castle, Richard decided to send an envoy, his half-brother the Duke of Exeter, to talk with Henry of Chester. Henry of Lancaster took from Exeter and the eleven horsemen who accompanied him his cognizances, the White Hart of King Richard, bestowing his own cognizances on him. When Exeter, the husband of Henry's sister Elizabeth, began to weep, the Earl of Rutland (created Duke of Aumerle by Richard II) said to him, "good cousin, do not vex yourself, for, please God, things will go well." All Henry's actions at this time indicate a predetermination to seize his cousin's throne.

Henry also sent two envoys, the Earl of Northumberland, then aged almost sixty, and ex-Archbishop Arundel, to Richard at Conway. It is evident that Northumberland intended to betray Richard, for he came to him with only seven attendants, having secretly concealed four hundred lancers and many archers in ambush in the mountains between Conway and Rhuddlan. Northumberland's terms were reasonable enough, if they had been genuine. The King might keep his throne provided he agreed to a free parliament, restored Henry's lands, and surrendered his friends, the Dukes of Exeter and Surrey, the Bishop of Carlisle and his own Clerk Maudelyn to Henry.

Northumberland was an unscrupulous nobleman, and it is obvious from the evidence that he would employ every wile to secure the King's person whether by persuasion or guile, so that he could deliver the King into the Duke of Lancaster's hands. What is far from certain is whether Bolingbroke had confided his intention to depose Richard to the nobleman, as Henry had sworn a solemn oath at Doncaster that he had no such intention. Northumberland is accused of swearing "upon the sacred body of our Lord" that his message from the Duke of Lancaster was true. In making such a solemn promise in the Chapel of Conway Castle after Mass, Northumberland perjured himself vilely. To the medieval mind to break a oath of this nature was a crime.

One of the illustrations in the Harleian manuscript shows the handsome old nobleman with his grey beard and dressed in his elaborate blue-star gown on his knees taking the oath. Far better for Richard if he had retreated to France where his own father-in-law Charles VI would have given him shelter. Instead, Richard decided to go to Flint Castle in North Wales to talk to his cousin Henry of Lancaster.

As he rode, somewhat apprehensively, with a few friends along the wild mountain paths, the glint of armour and spears soon convinced the King that he was betrayed. He was taken to Flint Castle, Northumberland's prisoner, captured by a despicable and shameful act of treachery. Northumberland left on horseback on Monday, August 21st for Chester to inform Henry that Richard had been captured. Henry rejoiced, ordering trumpets to be sounded and on the morrow he and his army, swollen from sixty to eighty thousand men, according to *Traison*, came to Flint.

For Henry it was a wonderful and proud moment as he rode along the beach, with his army beautifully deployed. For Richard as he watched from the battlements, it was truly agonizing, as Créton relates, seeing his hated cousin with this great host, their armour shining in the morning sun and the music of the minstrels coming strangely to his ears. According to Créton, who sympathized very strongly with Richard, "It was marvellously great (he is referring to the army) and showed such joy and satisfaction that the sound and bruit of their (musical) instruments, horns, buisines, were heard even as far as the Castle."

The French chronicler relates that many of the Duke's party entered Flint Castle, taunting Richard's followers. "Eat heartily, and make good cheer, for, by St. George, your heads will shortly be chopped off." Henry outwardly was very respectful to his cousin the King, bowing very low. Concealing the rancour in his heart, the King greeted Bolingbroke, "Fair cousin of Lancaster, ye are right welcome." The Duke of Lancaster replied, "My Lord, I am come before you sent for me; and I am come to help you to govern the kingdom of England, which you have not ruled well these twenty-two years...and therefore, with the consent of the Commons, I will help you to govern it." The Duke talked with the Bishop of Carlisle and others of the King's party, except for the Earl of Salisbury, saying that as little as he had deigned to speak to him when he was in Paris, so little would he speak to him now. Henry took Richard back to Chester where he was lodged in the Castle. How did Henry treat the King? There are conflicting accounts.

It is probable that Créton exaggerated the stories of Richard's ill treatment on the journey to London, but it is unlikely that Henry treated him *reverenter et honeste*. Richard was mounted on a horse "not worth thirty francs". Indignities were heaped on him. At Lichfield there was a serious attempt to rescue the King, but it failed. All the way to London, the Welsh and men of Cheshire inflicted much damage on Henry. Henceforward he was guarded as strictly as a thief or a murderer.

Both Froissart and Adam of Usk give different versions of a story that King Richard's favourite greyhound, Math, had already deserted the King for Henry. Froissart relates that "it alwaies wayted upon the King faune upon him and leape with his fore fote upon the Kynges shoulders, and as the Kynge and the Erle of Derby talked together in the Courte (of Flint Castle) the grayhounde left the King and came to the Duke of Lancaster and made to wyn the same continance and chere as he was want to do to the King." Richard said, "Cosyn it is a gret good token to you and an yvell signe to me." Henry, who was superstitious, as many people were in that late medieval age, took it as a good omen and welcomed the animal with joy, allowing the greyhound to sleep upon his bed. A greyhound was already one of Henry of Lancaster's badges.[32]

On reaching London, Henry left Richard in the custody of young Thomas of Gloucester, and Arundel (son of the executed Earl). He was hated by both these noblemen, and the mayor and chief citizens of London were determined to humiliate Richard. It was now September 1st. When a deputation of London aldermen had earlier advocated that Richard should be executed, Henry had refused their request, saying, "Fair Sirs, it would be a very great disgrace to us for ever, if we should thus put him to death; but we will bring him to London, and there he shall be judged by the Parliament." Writs had already been issued for the assembly of a Parliament to be held at Westminster on September 30th. After a night in the Palace of Westminster, Richard heard mass in the Abbey for the last time and was then escorted to the grim fortress of the Tower of London to the bitter curses of most of the people. For Henry there was a triumphant entry through the City of London, through Ludgate up to St. Paul's. All the way, there were shouts of "Long Live the Duke of Lancaster". At his father's tomb, Henry wept bitterly.

Henry's hereditary claim to Richard's throne rested on very weak foundations. He appointed a Commission "of sages in the law", including Adam of Usk, to scour the monasteries for evidence that Edmund Crouchback of Lancaster, his maternal ancestor, was in fact the elder brother of Edward I. Henry was doomed to disappointment, for their findings were completely negative. There was no substance to the Crouchback legend. He was forced to base his claim by right of conquest, although he obstinately adhered to the Crouchback story. However, the Commission did categorically state that "Richard's perjuries, sacrileges, unnatural crimes, exactions from his subjects, reductions of his people to slavery, cowardice and weakness of rule" were sufficient causes for deposing the King.

Archbishop Arundel, who had ousted Walden as Primate, favoured a plan whereby Richard would name Henry as his heir and willingly abdicate, influenced by the complaints of Parliament. Henry could then mount the throne as head of State to be controlled by Parliament. Everything would indicate that Richard was extremely reluctant to resign his throne. As a boy of ten he had been anointed with the sacred oil, and nobody could deprive him of that.

There is the terrible scene recorded by *Traison*[33] when Henry of Lancaster, the Duke of York and his son Edward of Rutland (recently Duke of Aumerle) visited the King in the Tower. Far from cheerfully acquiescing in yielding his crown, Richard accused both his uncle York and Rutland of being traitors. According to this account, when Rutland threw down his bonnet at his feet as a form of challenge, Richard replied passionately, "Traitor! I am King and thy Lord, and will still continue King and will be a greater lord than I ever was, in spite of all my enemies." Henry was very respectful to the King. When Richard asked for a fair trial, Henry merely said. "My Lord, be not afraid, nothing unreasonable shall be done to you." When Richard made the natural request that he should be allowed to see his queen - the child Isabelle - the Duke of Lancaster made the excuse: "It is forbidden by the Council." Several chronicles, including *The Dieulacres Chronicle* and *Giles Chronicle*, mention Richard's plea for a public trial. Some time during September, probably on September 29th, Richard was forced to resign his crown. The official version, Henry's parliament roll, is misleading, for there was no agreement by Richard at Conway to relinquish the throne.

Henry of Monmouth, Lancaster's heir, had been brought back from the Castle of Trim in Ireland by his father's orders during August or September. He seems to have had a genuine fondness for the King, rather than his father. Humphrey of Gloucester never reached England, for he died during the journey.

On September 30th one of the most important assemblies ever gathered together in Westminster Hall, composed of archbishops, bishops, dukes and earls, abbots and priors, citizens and burgesses. It was very tumultuous. This assembly cannot properly be described as a parliament because the King was not present, nor was there the customary opening speech of the Chancellor, or the appointment of a Speaker by the Commons or that of receivers and triers of petitions. Gaillard Lapsley discusses the Parliamentary title of Henry the Fourth.[34] Certainly the vacant throne was covered with cloth of gold, but there was no presiding officer. Sir William Thirnyng, Chief Justice of the Common Bench since 1396, played a prominent part in the proceedings and in his visits to King Richard in the Tower describes the persons who gathered in Westminster as "the estates".

What was grossly unfair was the denial of justice, the King not being allowed to speak in his own defence. If the official account can be believed, Richard had cheerfully accepted his abdication, but Adam of Usk, an eyewitness in the Tower, formed a very different impression a week earlier. The so-called "*gravimina*", the accusations reciting his misdeeds, were read in Latin and English. There were thirty-three articles. Among these many offences, he was accused of having the Duke of Gloucester murdered, he had broken oaths made to Thomas Arundel, Archbishop of Canterbury, and Henry of Lancaster; he had declared that "his lawes were in his mouthe" and of breaking his coronation oath. Of one charge there might be more justification. He was accused of illegally extracting loans, fines and blank charters from his subjects and causing them to be impoverished. There is one curious omission in the "*gravimina*", no accusation of Richard in relation to his handling of foreign affairs. True, there was a mention of the King's duplicity in that his foreign policy was intended to foster a domestic tyranny at home.

The "estates of the realm" after considering this heavy indictment, decided there was sufficient proof and now determined to pronounce sentence. Richard was declared "utterly unworthy and useless to rule and govern the realm."

Henry of Lancaster then stood up and everybody in that vast hall craned their necks to see him as he challenged the throne, wisely speaking in English, the first medieval King to do so when claiming the throne. "In the name of Fadir, Son and Holy Gost, I Henry of Lancastre, chalenge yis rewme of England and the Corone, with all ye membres and ye appurtenances ther to, als I yt am desendit (descended) be right lyne of the Blode Comyng fro the gude lorde Kyng Henry therde, and thorghe (through) yat ryght yat God of his grace hath sent me with helpe of my Kyn and 'of my Frendes to recover it, the which Rewme was in poynt' to ben undone, for defaut of governance and undoyng of the gode lawes."[35] But if Henry could have foreseen the anguish, the lack of peace and the constant burden of kingship, he might have been deterred from claiming the throne.

The lords and all the estates of the realm were then asked individually and collectively whether Henry should be king and agreed to it.

Henry's title to the throne was very weak, for the real hereditary heir was merely a boy, Edmund Mortimer, Earl of March, son of Roger Mortimer who had been killed at Kells. This is assuming that Roger Mortimer, descended from Lionel of Clarence, Edward III's third son, had been nominated Richard II's successor by parliament.

Thomas Arundel, now reinstated Archbishop of Canterbury, Henry's closest supporter, led him by the hand to the vacant throne and together with Richard Scrope, Archbishop of York, placed him upon it. He preached a short sermon, stressing the arguments that made children unfit to rule. No doubt he had Edmund Mortimer in mind, and also Richard, who had succeeded his grandfather Edward III at the tender age of ten.

Henry when thanking the lords spiritual and temporal, and "all the astates of the land", was careful to deny that "be waye of conquest I wold disherit any man of his heritage, franches, or other ryghtes that hym oght to have."

It was an act of significant courage for Thomas Merke, Bishop of Carlisle to rise and make a stout defence of Richard. The Lancastrian inspired Rolls of Parliament makes no mention of his speech, but the *Traison* alludes to it. "My lords, consider well before you give judgement upon what my lord the Duke has set forth, for I maintain that there is not one present who is competent and fit to judge such a soverign as my Lord the King whom we have acknowledged our (liege) lord for the space of twenty years and more...Moreover, I say that my Lord the Duke has more erred and offended against King Richard than has the King against him; for we know full well that my lord, the Duke was banished ten years by the Council of the realm, and by the consent of his own father, for the great crime which he and the Duke of Norfolk committed; and he has returned to the country without the King's permission, and moreover I say he has done still worse, for he has seated himself on the throne, where no man ought to sit other than the lawfully crowned King of England". Merke was immediately arrested and imprisoned, and subsequently deprived of his bishopric. Two years later he was pardoned. We do not hear of other protests, but there were many people in Westminster Hall gravely uneasy at the turn of events and Henry's acceptance of the crown.

On the following day Sir William Thirnyng and others visited Sir Richard of Bordeaux, as he was now known, in the Tower to inform him of his deposition, and that they had renounced their allegiance. Richard made one final objection, that he could not renounce the spiritual or mystical essence of his authority imparted to him at his coronation. Thirnyng argued that Richard had already owned that he was unworthy to reign. The deposed King swallowed his pride by saying: "I hope that myn cousin would be good lord to me."

Henry now decided that his coronation should be held on October 13th, a shrewd day to choose, for it marked the anniversary of the feast of the translation of St. Edward the Confessor, an important day for Westminster Abbey. Simultaneously Henry IV issued writs for a new parliament to assemble on Monday October 6th.

IV 'Uneasy lies the head'

On Sunday 12th October Henry IV at the Tower of London knighted his eldest son for the second time, together with his younger brothers and forty-five other persons. Henry was created Prince of Wales, Duke of Cornwall and Earl of Chester.[1] The new knights rode to Westminster with the King before his coronation. The traditional rites were followed, for the Sword of Justice he had carried as his father's deputy at Richard II's coronation was now borne by the Prince of Wales. The sword which the King had carried when he landed at Ravenspur, now known as the Lancaster sword, was borne by the Earl of Northumberland. Showing no sign of protest, Henry Percy played an important part in the King's coronation. King Henry's sinister friend Lord Grey of Ruthin carried the golden spurs without rowels.

For the superstitious there were at least two evil omens. After Henry IV had been anointed it was remarked that his head was swarming with lice. During the offertory, he dropped a gold noble, to be picked up by Adam of Usk. His coronation was followed by the customary banquet in Westminster Hall when the King's champion Sir Thomas Dymock, on horseback, challenged anyone bold enough to deny that Henry IV was not rightful King of England. Knowing the weakness of his title, the King said: "If need be, Sir Thomas, I will in mine own person ease thee of this office." He would not have been surprised if somebody present had made this challenge. One important nobleman, who is reputed to have refused to attend the coronation banquet, was Sir Harry Percy, the famous Hotspur, according to the *Dieulacres Chronicle*.

Adam of Usk relates that the deposed King disguised as a forester, and weeping bitter tears, was carried by night on the Thames, crying that he regretted ever having been born. He was taken to Leeds Castle, where his wretched plight reminded him of happier days in that beautiful castle. From Leeds he was removed on October 25th to Gravesend in Kent, according to some chronicles, and from there to Pontefract Castle in West Yorkshire. With its great keep and its many turrets, this fortress was to be Richard's prison for several months. Its custodian was Sir Thomas Swynford, Henry's stepbrother and close companion in arms but Richard's bitter enemy and he is likely to have received harsh treatment. Henry was plagued with a terrible problem at the beginning of his reign: what to do with his prisoner, and there were not wanting among his advisers those who tried to persuade him to put him to death. Only an armed rising would force Henry to agree to such a desperate course.

From the first, Henry was only too aware that he was an usurper, and constantly gave the impression throughout his reign of thirteen-and-a-half years that he was at the mercy of events, not in control of them. The weakness of his title made him subservient to his parliaments, but he did have the good sense to establish amicable relations with parliament. Mindful that Richard II had too often been influenced by his favourites, Henry was careful to give a general promise at the beginning of his reign that he would not govern alone, but with the help of wise counsellors.[2] Unlike Richard, he behaved in a very conciliatory way on a number of occasions. For instance, in 1404 the Commons asked the King to remove some members of his household and he agreed, perhaps reluctantly, to do so. Parliament was very jealous of its rights to grant taxation, and on several occasions when this right was threatened, Henry deferred to them. He was jealous, however, of his prerogative to appoint his own ministers.

He was, for instance, very attached to his close friend John Norbury, whom he appointed Treasurer of England on September 3rd before his coronation, influenced no doubt by the fact that Norbury's daughter Joan was married to William Parker, Alderman and Mercer of the City of London. Henry trusted Norbury whether in or out of office, granting him Leeds Castle for life. We find him writing to Ralph Neville, Earl of Westmoreland, referring to the recovery of the King from an illness, and to Archbishop Arundel concerning the capture of the rebel lords such as the Earl of Huntingdon and Lord Despenser, who had risen on behalf of Richard II during December 1399. As Treasurer Norbury lent the

Exchequer £666, and during October summoned all the Collectors of Customs to the Exchequer, hoping that money would be found for the wars in Scotland and Wales.[3]

Financially, Henry was a complete failure, not altogether his fault because Parliament seldom granted him sufficient money, constantly reminding him that he was an usurper. However, his first duty was to restore and maintain financial stability and he signally failed to do so.[4]   Richard II had levied arbitrary taxes, but his successor failed to remedy the situation, for the royal debt during his reign was swollen to enormous proportions owing to a series of annual deficits. Many people had hailed Henry's succession only to be gravely disappointed. Far from bringing peace and prosperity, Henry's reign brought many baronial rebellions, cruel wars in Wales and Scotland, and widespread discontent.

The first baronial rebellion was a rising of Richard II's friends during December 1399. Several chronicles, including *The Brut*[5] and *La Traison*, give their accounts. *The Brut* relates: "And yn the first yare of King Henryes reigne he hilde his Christmasse yn the Castell of Wyndesore, and on the twelfth evyn came the Duke of Awmaile unto the King and tolde hym that he and the Duke of Surrey, the Duke of Excestre, the Erle of Salisbury, and the Erle of Gloucester...were accorded to make a mummyng unto the King on the fifteenth day at nyght". Their plan was to slay the King and his sons.

These Dukes had actually been degraded by the King. Known now by their former titles of Rutland and Huntingdon, apparently Abbot William Colchester of Westminster had invited these disaffected nobles on December 17th 1399 to dine with him at the Abbey, for his sympathies and those of the monks strongly favoured Richard II. Among the conspirators were the Earl of Salisbury, Lord Despenser, Thomas Merke, no longer bishop of Carlisle, Roger Walden the displaced Archbishop of Canterbury, and Richard Maudelyn, who bore a remarkable resemblance to the former King, Master Pol, Richard's physician, and Sir Thomas Blount, a knight always loyal to Richard. They were to assemble at Kingston-on-Thames (formerly known as Kingeston) on January 4th 1400 with a small armed force and ride by night to Windsor. Here other plotters would overpower the guards and

Henry and his sons would be killed. According to the *Sloane manuscript*, an extraordinary instrument called a 'caltrappe' had been put in Henry's bed for the purpose of destroying him. It seems incredible considering Rutland's reputation for double-dealing, that he should be trusted by his fellow conspirators. Sure enough he betrayed the plot to his father Edmund of Langley, Duke of York, who informed the King.

Henry was always at his best if a situation demanded rapid action. Summoning his sons, he galloped with them to London. Within two days he had collected an army of 20,000 men. This was remarkable promptness for dealing with an extremely dangerous situation, since he and the young Prince of Wales had been ill at Windsor, probably owing to attempts to poison them. *La Traison* gives a full account of how the conspirators arrived at Windsor too late, and of their subsequent fate after raising an army of several thousands. The Earls of Salisbury and Kent were captured by the mob at Cirencester and were immediately beheaded, while eighty other rebels were taken in arms and tried at Oxford, among them Sir Thomas Blount, who was executed, and thirty others. Their bodies were taken to London, their salted heads in baskets, to be displayed on London Bridge. Henry's brother-in-law, the Earl of Huntingdon, was captured at Prithwell in Essex and executed at Pleshey, owing to the vindictive Joan Countess of Hereford, Henry IV's mother-in-law, a sister of the executed Earl of Arundel. When Archbishop Arundel, his younger brother, sang the Te Deum at St. Paul's, he gave thanks to the Virgin Mary "for rescuing the most christian king from the fangs of wolves and the jaws of wild beasts, who had prepared above their backs a gallows mixed with gall and hated as with a bitter hate."[6]

Tradition says that Richard was confined at Pontefract in a narrow wretched chamber containing two very small windows. Owing to the rebellion of his friends, his life was doomed. Henry at first had resisted the urging of leading barons that the deposed king should be put to death, but Henry could know no security while his cousin remained alive. It is almost certain that Richard was murdered or starved to death, and such documentary evidence as we possess would signify that there existed a Council order known to the King decreeing his death. No credence should be attached to the story in *La Traison* that Sir Peter Exton was the assassin, by an axe blow on his head, also used in Shakespeare's *Tragedy of Richard II*. The most probable cause of death was forcible starvation. Richard was certainly dead by February 14th 1400. Adam of Usk definitely states that the starvation was imposed and that Sir Thomas Swynford tormented the King "with starving fare". Suggestive evidence that Richard's murder was carefully planned is contained among the exchequer payments. "To William Loveney, Clerk of the Great Wardrobe, sent to Pontefract Castle on secret business by order of the King (Henry IV) 66s.8d.[7] Richard's body lay at St. Paul's for two days with his face exposed, and parts of his body were buried at the Dominican priory of King's Langley in Hertfordshire, a palace beloved by Richard and his Queen Anne and where his elder brother, Edward of Angoulême, had also been buried. Rumours, however, that Richard was still alive in Scotland were to trouble King Henry for most of his reign.

As Earl of Derby, Henry had never been troubled by financial worries, but as King his income was never sufficient for his needs. He was constantly forced to borrow and he was far less conscientious than Richard II in repaying his creditors. His good fortune did not outlast his usurpation of his cousin's throne. There was a rapid decline in the volume of wool, England's chief export. Whereas the annual revenue from the custom and subsidy on wool had remained fairly constant at £47,000 for the twenty-two years of Richard's reign and £43,000 for the last three years, Henry was unfortunate in that it fell to £39,000 in the first three years of his reign. In 1401-1403 there were a series of very wet summers, causing a fall in the number of sheep. For a while the revenue from the custom and subsidy on wool fell to £26,000, though there was a partial recovery of £36,000 per annum during the last period of his thirteen year reign.[8] Henry had made rash promises to reduce taxation, which he could not honour, nor could he reward his followers as lavishly as he desired. His early popularity began to wane rapidly. He certainly did not bring peace or stability to the kingdom, for much of his reign was torn by constant riots and rebellion.

Authors are today deeply indebted to Wylie's massive researches and book about *The Reign of Henry IV*, but to assert as he does that the King cannot be fairly charged with advancing to kingship by 'crokked by-paths' is not true.[9]

Adam of Usk's chronicle is full of strange incidents and omens. For instance, he relates that during 1400 four little bells hanging at the corners of shrine in Westminster Abbey, rang of their own accord "and with more than human power, miraculously sounded four times on one day, to the great awe and wonder of the brethren." That year was an unhappy time in England, when a cursed plague caused havoc in the land, killing many people. Superstitious people said it was God's judgement for the wickedness in high places. The chronicler Grafton, writing in the time of Elizabeth I, mentions a comet appearing during the following year, "a blazing starre of a great and huge qualitie which expounded to signifye great effusion of mans' blood, and the same proved true."

Henry's most influential adviser for many years was Archbishop Arundel who had helped him to the throne. His political sagacity sustained Henry when he was threatened by enemies, but during his meteoric career he was much concerned, even when Bishop of Ely (1381), in attempting to prevent the spread of heresy and unorthodox preaching. He was responsible for persuading Henry to introduce the iniquitous statute *De Heretico Comburendo* (January 1401) whereby bishops could surrender obstinate heretics to the secular authority to be burnt alive. To be fair to Arundel, he always attempted to make the heretics brought before him recant.[10] Such an offender was William Sautre, a Lollard priest from Norfolk, who had been examined by the Bishop of Norwich in 1399 and made to renounce his beliefs. After he had resumed his heretical teachings, he was arrested and brought before Archbishop Arundel and condemned to a horrible death at Smithfield. One does not hear of any protests by the vast crowd gathered at Smithfield to see the wretched man die: "chained standing to a post in a barel packed round with blazing faggots." Henry IV being strictly orthodox as to his religion, would have favoured Arundel's views.

Political troubles assailed Henry from every direction when he mounted the throne. As might be expected, Charles VI of France, subject to intermittent fits of insanity, and Richard II's father-in-law, was hostile to Henry. France looked upon him as an usurper and would not recognize him. Henry had used Richard's

Queen Isabelle's dowry for his own pressing financial needs, and made overtures for a possible marriage between her and the Prince of Wales, aged thirteen in 1400, but the French now demanded the restoration of Richard's child-widow. Negotiations for her return were protracted, partly owing to Henry's desire to retain Isabelle as a hostage in case of French attack. France indeed was riven by factiousness, mainly because of Charles VI's incapacity to govern, and the rivalry between his brother Louis of Orléans and his uncle Philip the Bold (*Le Hardi*), Duke of Burgundy. This rivalry between Orléans and Burgundy was of considerable importance for thirty years, because English foreign policy was to play them off one against another.[11]

Scotland also presented a perpetual problem. Her King in 1400 was Robert III of the Stuart family, a poor statesman. Despite intermittent border warfare, a truce existed between the two countries. *The Royal and Historical Letters, Henry IV*, contains a letter from Henry to Robert written towards the end of 1396 reminding him of the truce, and another one written probably in November 1399 after his accession, complaining that he had not received any satisfactory answer to his previous letter "alluding to the great and horrible outrages committed by the sons of Scottish wardens." Robert's habit of addressing Henry in a letter written on November 2nd 1399 as 'Duke of Lancaster, Count of Derby and Seyeschal of England', must have angered him considerably.

During February 1400 George Dunbar, the Scottish Earl of March, felt so insulted by Robert's son, the Duke of Rothesay's rejection of his daughter, that he decided to espouse Henry's cause.[12] For that purpose the King shrewdly instructed his brother-in-law Ralph Neville, Earl of Westmoreland (he had married Joan Beaufort, Henry's half sister) to treat with George Dunbar.[13] The Scottish Earl of March, a skilful soldier, was later invaluable to Henry, both at the Battle of Homildon Hill fighting with Hotspur, and also advising Henry at the Battle of Shrewsbury (1403).

The most dangerous rebellion against Henry's rule was that of the Percys in the same year. This famous family was at the zenith of its power and influence at the end of Richard's reign, holding large estates in Yorkshire, Northumberland and Cumberland, the most powerful magnates on the Scottish border. There is evidence that Henry, first Percy Earl of Northumberland, and his son Hotspur, were on bad terms with Richard II for various reasons, particularly because the King had granted the Penrith estates in Cumberland to their great rival Ralph Neville, Earl of Westmoreland.

There is no doubt also that Northumberland and Hotspur had given Henry invaluable military support, so that Bolingbroke could seize Richard's crown and gain possession of the kingdom. What is far more difficult to ascertain is their real motives for supporting Henry. Hotspur declared three years later that he had rebelled because of the crown which the King had unjustly seized and which should have passed by hereditary right to the son of the Earl of March (described through the female line, Philippa daughter of the Duke of Clarence). As already related, Hotspur had refused to attend the coronation banquet, according to the *Dieulacres Chronicle*, confirming the charge that Duke Henry had solemnly sworn on the relics of Bridlington that he would never seek the crown, and alleged to have said that if anyone more worthy of the crown was found, he would willingly withdraw.[14] The *Dieulacres Chronicle* locates Henry's oath at Bridlington, not Doncaster. Hardyng's chronicle exists in two versions - the Lancastrian, presented to Henry VI, Henry IV's grandson, and the Yorkshire, presented to Edward IV. The only version in print, the Yorkist version, favours the Percy manifesto of 1403 that Henry had himself crowned king, despite the attempts of the three Percys to make him keep to his oath. It is fair to add, however, that Hardyng as a faithful retainer of his master Hotspur, is often biased in favour of the Percys. Thomas Percy, Earl of Worcester, according to the *Chronique de la Traison*, at a parliament in London, cried 'Long live Henry of Lancaster, King of England.' Whether it was a properly constituted parliament is far more doubtful. This chronicle mentions the Earl of Northumberland as amongst the lords urging Henry to put Richard to death a few months later after the first rebellion of his reign.

The Percys undoubtedly made handsome gains on Henry's accession. Northumberland on September 30th became Constable of England for life and also Warden of the West March in the north, and Hotspur, Warden of the East March. On October 24th the castle and lordship of Bamburgh Castle were granted to Hotspur for life, while the Earl of Northumberland received the Isle of Man on October 19th 1399. Hotspur also benefited from various grants in Chester and North Wales, becoming Justice of Chester, North Wales and given the Constableships of the castles of Chester, Conway, Caernarvon and Flint; the lordships of Anglesey and Beaumaris Castle. On his part the Earl of Worcester was given 500 marks a year for life, created Admiral of England, having all the grants received from Edward III and Richard II confirmed.[15]

Despite this apparent generosity of Henry IV, the Percys were soon to have genuine grievances against the King, mainly financial, because of the heavy expenses incurred in their arduous work in the Marches. The various reasons for their rebellion will be discussed later.

As king, now aged thirty-four, Henry was hard-working, active and trustful of his friends, but he had a hot temper. On the whole he was merciful and the courtiers even deplored his clemency, urging him to behave more ruthlessly but in any case he had a cruel streak. Not an easy man to love, for bitter experience had gradually taught him to be reserved and suspicious. Henry had an excellent brain and a retentive memory, finding great pleasure in the conversation of men of letters. His father was more to be esteemed as a patron, but Henry doubled Geoffrey Chaucer's pension, although he died in 1400, a year after Bolingbroke's accession. Hoccleve, an admirer of Henry IV and of Henry V, was rewarded by the King more as a civil servant, being a clerk in the privy seal office, than as a poet. John Gower, who had deserted Richard II for the Earl of Derby, flattered Henry in some verses on his accession:

> Thus tellen thei whiche olde bookes canne
> Whereof, my lord, y wot wel thou art lerned.[16]

It is not recorded that Gower received a financial reward.

Henry delighted in the poetry of Christine de Pisan, biographer of Charles V of France. Her son had been in England, a guest of the cultured Earl of Salisbury, friend of Richard II, and

Henry tried to persuade Christine to join his court, without success. Henry was himself cultured, well educated and fond of quoting Latin and he wrote well in English. He was extremely musical and his interest in music remained constant, as it was in his early life with Mary de Bohun already mentioned. It has been suggested that Henry was the 'Henry Roy', who composed a *Gloria in Excelsis* and other church music in the early fifteenth century.[17] In Shakespeare's play *Henry IV* the King, unable to woo sleep, "Nature's soft nurse",[18] envies those lying on uneasy pallets to whom it comes. Even when "lull'd with sound of sweetest melody" sleep still eludes him.

As king, Henry was fond of staying in his palace at Eltham, near London (his favourite palace). It was here that he entertained the Emperor Manuel II of Palaeologus of Constantinople, who was in desperate need of Western help against the Turks, a continual threat to his kingdom. During Christmas 1400, Henry entertained Manuel to jousting. There is a letter in Latin written five months earlier from Peter Holt, Prior of the Hospital of Saint John of Jerusalem in Ireland, to Manuel II, who was at that time in Paris, advising him to defer his visit since King Henry was in Scotland.[19] He was attempting to force Robert III to pay homage. All the more gratifying was a letter from his second cousin Albert, Count of Hainault, pledging his support. He was the father of William of Hainault, who had once invited Henry to join him in the war against Friesland, but John of Gaunt had forbidden him to go.

The short reign of Henry IV was of significant importance for the development of parliament. There was no premature flowering of a democratic system as Bishop Stubbs alleges. Parliaments, however, took every opportunity to criticize the King, and realizing that he needed money, enabled Parliament to make demands on the price for granting taxation. When Henry made difficulties, he could always be reminded that he was an usurper.

About this time special privileges for members of Parliament and their servants were granted. From then onwards members were secure from personal molestation or even arrest. There is the special case of Richard Cheddar,[20] a member of Parliament's servant, beaten and wounded by a man named John Savage.

Savage was ordered to surrender in the King's Bench, and in default to pay double damages, besides being fined.

The Speaker chosen for Henry's second Parliament held at Westminster from January 20th 1401 until March 20th, was Sir Arnold Savage, a former Sheriff of Kent during Richard's reign, a rather verbose man and known for his boring speeches, but one of Henry's early advisers. When Parliament requested the King to institute a painstaking inquiry into the inventory of the deposed King Richard's jewels, Henry denied ever receiving any of them. He declared that he was poor and needy. In this Parliament, harsh action was taken against the Lollards. When the King was hectored by Sir Arnold Savage to change some of his ministers and to name his councillors, he did not yield, only giving way on minor points. However, the King was granted his money, but obliged by the request of the Commons to remove some aliens from the Council. The severe repressive legislation against the Welsh, included in a statute for Wales, served to exasperate that mountain race, limiting the rights of Welshmen resident in England, protecting Englishmen from Welsh Juries, and declaring that for three years no Englishman was to be indicted or accused by the Welsh.

During the summer of 1400 Henry IV and his son the Prince of Wales were engaged in a campaign in Scotland, only to hear on their return that a rebellion had broken out in Wales. Early in October, the King and his eldest son went to Wales on a punitive expedition, and on their return Prince Henry, now thirteen, remained at Chester with a Council headed by Harry Hotspur. Prince Henry was to serve his apprenticeship as a soldier in Wales under this highly experienced warrior, now aged thirty-four, "no infant Mars", as Shakespeare calls him, using dramatic licence. That Prince Henry was to become a great soldier during the hard Welsh wars lasting eight years was to some extent his good fortune in having Hotspur as his mentor.

There were many reasons for the Welsh rebellion of 1400, led by a great guerrilla leader, Owain Glyn Dŵr. The main reason was Henry IV's lack of statesmanship in handling the Welsh problem, a very complex one. He showed no imaginative understanding of his Welsh subjects, nor did he want to, for he despised them at heart. If he really said, "What care we for these barefooted scrubs", his character is seen in an unfavourable light. John Trevor, Bishop of St. Asaph, a Welshman, who was with Richard in Ireland in August 1399 before deserting to Henry, warned the English parliament of their folly in ill-treating the Welsh. In 1405 he was to desert to Owain Glyn Dŵr. Another grievance and cause of discontent was Henry IV's unwise attempt to exact heavy communal payments from his Welsh subjects. It was customary for these communal payments to be exacted at the accession of a monarch. Richard II had also made levies, but he had enjoyed some popularity in North Wales. Henry was undoubtedly resented because of his usurpation of Richard's throne. The arrogant Marcher lords, mainly interested in augmenting their incomes and trampling on peoples' rights, were deeply unpopular, being regarded as alien landlords. Again Welshmen felt frustrated because they were often excluded from high office in secular and ecclesiastical appointments. Throughout this major revolt, the last uprising against the Anglo-Norman conquest of Wales, there existed a marked diversity of rebel motives and divisions in Welsh society. Consequently, however patriotic it might seem, it was only partly a national rebellion.

It is unfortunate that in 1402 Adam of Usk, a Welshman, had been forced to depart abroad, having been found guilty of stealing a black horse and some money in London in 1400, for he could have given us much more firsthand information about Owain's rebellion if he had remained in England.

V   The Welsh Rebellion

Its immediate cause in 1400 was the quarrel between Owain Glyn
Dŵr, a rich Welsh landowner, with Reginald Lord Grey of Ruthyn,
an aggressive Marcher Lord and intimate friend of Henry IV.[1]
Reginald Grey had espoused Henry's cause and had been present
at his coronation. He was in fact an intimate friend, and during the
ceremony had carried the golden spurs without rowels before they
were buckled over the King's crimson velvet slippers. Grey's
quarrel with the Welshman concerned some lands claimed by
Owain, as part of his inheritance, and forcibly seized by Lord
Grey. His lands lay in the valley of the Clwyd between Denbigh
and Flint in North Wales, and Owain's lands bordered Grey's.
Seeking a just solution in their quarrel, Owain travelled to London
to petition parliament and the King, but he was given no satisfaction. Burning with resentment, he returned to Wales.

Henry's choice of Lord Grey to deal with the Welsh, a
difficult and factious race, could not have been worse, for he was
openly contemptuous of the people. Early in 1400 there was
already some disorder in Wales. Grey of Ruthyn was engaged in
a dispute with a man named Griffith ap David ap Griffith, who
incensed at not receiving the office of bailiff of Chirkland, had
trespassed onto Lord Grey's lands and stolen two of his horses.
There followed a letter from Griffith to his adversary protesting
his innocence and that he was the victim of treachery. The bitter
feeling between Wales and England mounted. Griffith might be a
rude, even a barbaric man, but Lord Grey lacked all pretence of
diplomacy and courtesy in his dealings with Griffith, who at least
ended his letter with the civil hope, "Gode keepe your worshipfull
astate in prosperite." In his reply Grey wrote in mocking, mali-
cious verse to the Welshman:

> but we hoope we shalle do the a pryve thyng
> A roope, a ladder, and a ring

Heigh on gallowes for to henge,
And thus shall be your endyng.[2]

To the Prince of Wales, Grey referred to Griffith as "the strengest thiefe in Wales".

It is said that Owain Glyn Dŵr had been summoned by King Henry to take part in the Scottish campaign during the summer (1400) but Lord Grey, from motives of sheer malice, had failed to deliver the summons, wanting to make it appear that Owain was a traitor. The exact date of the birth of the great Welsh rebel is very uncertain. Thomas Pennant in his *Tours of Wales* favours May 28th 1354, but in the records of the celebrated Scrope-Grosvenor Trial (1386) during Richard II's reign, when Glyn Dŵr was a witness, it was stated that he was twenty-seven or more, so 1359 may be more likely.

His family held large estates, the Glen of Water of Dee, lying between Llangollen and Corwen, his home a lovely place named Sycharth, described by the Welsh poet Iolo Goch as an idyllic haven of peace and prosperity. A moat with a bridge and sparkling water surrounded it. His father, Griffith, content to live a quiet life, was descended from Welsh princes, and his mother Helen also came of a princely family. In his early career Owain studied law at Westminster, joining an Inn of Court for seven years. He then became a soldier, entering the service of Henry of Lancaster, the future Henry IV, and probably serving under Richard Fitzalan, Earl of Arundel (later beheaded), who owned valuable estates in north-east Wales. Further military experience was acquired during Richard II's wars in Scotland.

His physical appearance has seldom been described, but he was a tall and handsome man with long reddish-brown hair curling outwards, almost brushing his shoulders; a striking personality, cultured and even learned, and he sported a beard. He had a wart under his left eye. Owain married Margaret Hanmer of Maelor, daughter of an illustrious Welshman and a judge during the reign of Edward III. Happily married, they had a large family of six sons and several daughters.

Owain proclaimed himself Prince of Wales, but the simple ceremony lacked the pomp attending the investiture of Henry,

Prince of Wales. His raid on Ruthyn with its imposing red castle in north-east Wales was a total success, for the town, then an important cloth and shoe market, was severely damaged and many buildings destroyed. For Glyn Dŵr it was sweet revenge on his enemy Lord Grey, for he held the castle and outside the walls lay his orchards and fish ponds. Emboldened by success, the Welsh marched from Rhuddlan to Flint, burning and looting Denbigh, Hawarden and other towns. King Henry acted with decision when he first heard of the rebellion in Northampton, marching to Lichfield from Coventry on September 22nd (1400) and then to Shrewsbury, where he assembled an impressive army. With the Prince of Wales he moved to Bangor on the Menai Straits, where various abbots hastened to submit to the King. However, the bitter feeling between the rebels and the loyalists was too strong. After Rhys Tudor, one of Owain's lieutenants, attacked the royal family at Rhos Faror, near the castle of Beaumaris, Henry in revenge destroyed the Franciscan house of Llanfaes.

During the fifteenth century war was a trade, ravage its handmaid and human life was of small account.[3] Both English and Welsh indulged in frightful pillaging and plunder of towns. Adam of Usk, who was by no means unsympathetic to Owain, describes him "like a second Assyrian harrying town and countryside with fire and sword, carrying off the spoil of the land and specially cattle to the mountains of Snowdon". A superb guerrilla leader, avoiding pitched battles wherever possible, Henry IV was no match for him. His campaigns in 1400 and October 1401 met with ignominious failure. There are indications that Owain only became a rebel from necessity. He had been wrongfully deprived of his lands and if they had been returned to him he might have sought a peaceful settlement. However, among Henry's advisers were the implacable Lord Grey and other hard men, who would have resisted any peace overtures.

During Easter 1401 Owain's cousins Rhys and Gwilym ap Tudor, natives of the Isle of Anglesea, heard that Conway Castle in North Wales was neglectfully guarded. The garrison consisted of fifteen men-at-arms and sixty archers under the command of John Massy of Podynton. On Good Friday, while most of the garrison were at church, a Welshman disguised as a carpenter entered the castle, followed by Gwilyn ap Tudor and forty doughty soldiers, who swiftly overpowered the warders. Conway Castle fell into the hands of the Welsh.

Harry Hotspur, Chief Justice of North Wales and keeper of the Lordship of Denbigh, now aged thirty-five, with a force of 120 men and 300 archers immediately galloped to Conway. Accompanied by Henry Prince of Wales, he prepared for a long siege of Conway Castle, and Rhys and Gwilyn Tudor eventually submitted. A letter exists from King Henry to the Prince of Wales thanking him and Henry Percy for "their great pain and diligence"[4], revealing at least that in 1401 he was on amicable terms with his eldest son. Although Rhys and Gwilyn's lives were spared, nine[5] of their companions were betrayed into the hands of the English while they slept, to be brutally beheaded and quartered. The siege had been costly and King Henry persuaded the Council to refund Hotspur and the Prince £200. It is doubtful whether it was ever paid. Meanwhile Hotspur at his own expense organized his troops against a rebel army operating in the neighbourhood of Dalgelly.

Wales was an unlucky country for Henry IV. Richard II had enjoyed some popularity in North Wales, but Henry had no reason to like the country. As Shakespeare relates in the mouth of Glyn Dŵr:

> Three times hath Henry Bolingbroke made head
> against my power; thrice from the banks of Wye
> and sandy-bottomed Severn have I sent him
> Bootless home and weather-beaten back.

Henry can seldom have slept soundly in his tent, fearing assassination and attempts to kill him. Capgrave the contemporary chronicler, relates that Henry's tent was once blown down in the night, and he only escaped serious injury because he laid down in his armour. Another medieval chronicler tells a story: "In the vigils of the nativities of oure lady, the kyng had picchid his tent in a fayr pleyne, there blew sudeynly so much wynd and so impetuous with a great rayn, that the kyngis tent was felled, and a spare cast so violently that had the kyng not been armed, he had been ded of the stroke."

As Hardyng relates: "The king had never but tempest foule and raine as long as he was in Wales." The atrocious climate was Owain's best ally. When hurricanes of hail, wind and rain descended on the hapless English, they swore in their awe-struck way that Glyn Dŵr was a wizard and could change the weather according to his whim by an incantation.

The ruins of the lovely Cistercian Abbey of Strata Florida, fourteen miles from Aberystwyth, lies in an entrancing valley. Throughout its long and fascinating history, the Cistercian monks had been constantly loyal to their Welsh princes, so King Henry, seeking revenge, ordered the Abbey to be plundered and even allowed his knights to stable their horses at the high altar. According to Adam of Usk, the English invaded these parts during the autumn (1401) "ravaging them with fire, famine and sword, not even sparing Strata Florida and carrying away into England a thousand children to be their servants."

Later in 1407, the Abbey provided barrack accommodation for 120 English men-at-arms and 360 archers. Today all is peace and one can but marvel at the beauty and grace of the tile pavements. Beside the Abbey is buried Dafydd ap Gwilyn, the Welsh poet, who died about 1370, known for his poems on nature and love.

On leaving Wales in late 1401, Henry IV had commissioned Thomas Percy, Earl of Worcester, his lieutenant in South Wales for three months, a wise appointment since Hotspur's uncle was a fine soldier. From October 21st, Worcester had pursued a policy of conciliation with some success, especially in Cardiganshire. Towards the end of 1401 he wrote to the Prince of Wales to say that Glyn Dŵr was prepared to parley with Henry, but his ambassadors would not submit to the King's grace for fear of their lives.[6]

Hotspur's own opinions were conciliatory, like his uncle's. From 1401 onwards he nursed mounting grievances against Henry IV, complaining that the troops in Berwick and in the East Marches of Wales had not been paid. In the West Marches they had suffered the same fate for several months. On May 2nd he wrote from Caernarvon that the troops in the East Marches were in such distress that they could not endure for lack of money. Denbigh Castle, where Hotspur was mainly stationed, lies in a magnificent position in the heart of the Vale of Clwyd, a castle built by Henry de Lacy, Earl of Lincoln, Edward I's Chief Commander in Wales. From his headquarters he wrote stressing the great labours and expenses he had incurred in the King's service and the necessity to provide sufficient funds in Wales. From the tone in Harry Percy's letters, it is evident that he blamed some hostile influence in the Council, possibly Ralph Neville, Earl of Westmoreland, his father's hereditary enemy, rather than the King himself. Were Hotspur and his father shabbily treated by Henry IV?

Between October 1399 and July 1403 the Percys received in cash or in assignment sums not far short of £50,000.[7] This can scarcely be described as niggardly. Where father and son were justified in their complaints can be explained in that assignments were often made over in so-called tallies, difficult to realize in cash. For instance, on December 2nd 1402 Harry Percy sent into the Exchequer of Receipt eight tallies amounting to £4,115, since he had been refused payment of these tallies by the accountants. Of the £50,000 originally advanced to Northumberland and his son, as much as £10,778 consisted of "bad tallies". Eventually, his patience exhausted, Hotspur always impetuous, resigned his onerous posts as Justician of North Wales, as guardian of the Prince of Wales and his other offices, to return to the border country to assist his father in his efforts to preserve peace with the Scots. Unlike the Marcher Lords, such as Lord Grey of Ruthyn, who had landed wealth in Wales, the Percys favoured a more conciliatory policy towards Owain, even a settlement whereby concessions would be granted Glyn Dŵr and some of their grievances remedied on condition that they returned their allegiance to King Henry. The Percys had nothing to lose in Wales, for their landed estates were all in Northumberland and Yorkshire. That Hotspur was later engaged in intrigues with Owain is certain, because one of his squires, William Lloyd of Denbigh, travelled to Berwick during April 1403 to confer with his master, carrying the threads of an intrigue.

King Henry had strongly criticized his predecessor for his tyrannous rule, but his own confessor, Philip Repyndon, was bold enough to send Henry a letter of remonstrance during 1401, complaining about the state of the kingdom. "For law and justice are banished from the realm, thefts, murders, adulteries, fornications, extortions, oppressions of the poor, hurts, wrongs, and much reproach are rife and one tyrant will both serve for law."[8] Repyndon was not only Henry's confessor, but also his chaplain and friend, and the King had asked his confessor to speak to him frankly. Formerly Repyndon had been a staunch follower of Wycliffe, but he had abjured in 1382. For ten years he was Abbot of the monastery of St. Mary de Pré at Leicester. He did not suffer for his frankness, for he became Bishop of Lincoln in 1405 for fourteen years. Henry helped his career, since Pope Gregory XII created him a cardinal in 1408.

The negotiations for the return of Richard's young Queen Isabelle, not yet eleven, to France, had been protracted, for Henry had refused to surrender her dowry to keep his exchequer solvent. She was never popular in England. Her own household had cost nearly £3,000[9] during the first year of Henry's reign and her journey to be restored to her father Charles VI required considerable ceremonial. Adam of Usk describes (June 28th 1401) Isabelle "clad in mourning weeds and showing a countenance of lowering and evil aspect to King Henry" on returning to France. She believed him to have been King Richard's murderer. Adam heard the people muttering that the little Queen would bring further troubles on England because of her craving for vengeance for her husband's death. Among those escorting her to France were Thomas Percy, Earl of Worcester, the King's mother-in-law, the Countess of Hereford, and the Duchess of Ireland, widow of Richard's favourite, Robert de Vere. Devoted to his memory, her life was unhappy. She married the Count of Angoulême in 1406, who became Duke of Orléans on the murder of his father Louis in Paris but she was to die in childbirth in 1409.

If Louis of Orléans' sentiments towards Henry of Lancaster had ever been sincere or friendly before Henry usurped Richard's throne, they were certainly hostile now. The chronicle of Enguerrand de Monstrelet, an important French chronicler who sprang from a noble family and was probably a nobleman of Picardy,[10] contains scornful correspondence between Henry and Orléans. Orléans wrote: "In regard to your ignorance or pre-

Henry IV by an unknown artist.

The Jousts of St. Inglevert near Calais in which Henry of Bolingbroke and his knights took part.

The impressive, fortified palace and monastery of the Teutonic Knights, well known to Henry of Bolingbroke.

Henry IV being crowned by the Archbishops of Canterbury and York.

Owain Glyn Dŵr, Welsh Prince of Wales.

Effigy of the Usurper King at Canterbury Cathedral.

tended ignorance whether my letter could have been addressed to you, your name was on it, such as you received at the font, and by which you were always called by your parents when they were alive...In regard to your being surprised at my requesting to perform a deed of arms with you during the existence of the truce between my most redoubted lord the King of France and the high and mighty Prince King Richard my nephew and your liege lord lately deceased (God knows by whose orders) as well as an alliance of friendship subsisting between us, of which you have sent me a copy - that treaty is now at an end by your own fault, first by your having undertaken your enterprise against your Sovereign Lord King Richard (whom God pardon!)...I do not think the divine virtues have placed you there...you say, you shall be always eager to defend your honour which has ever been unblemished. Enough on that head is sufficiently known in all countries. How could you suffer my much redoubted lady the Queen of England (Isabelle) to return so desolate to this country after the death of her lord, despoiled by your rigour and cruelty of her dower, which you detain from her and likewise the portion she carried here on her marriage." Orléans wrote to Henry from the Castle of Coucy, once the residence of Enguerrand, Lord of Coucy, the husband of Isabelle, eldest daughter of Edward III.

Henry defended himself from these accusations: "God knows from whom nothing can be concealed that so far from acting towards her harshly we have ever shown her kindness and friendship and whoever shall dare say otherwise lies wickedly." Referring to her money, he added that it was notorious that on leaving this kingdom he had made her such restitution of jewels and money ("much more than she brought here") that we hold ourselves acquitted.

In his lifetime Louis of Orléans had a rather unsavoury reputation and was probably one of the lovers of Isabeau of Bavaria, Charles VI's wanton queen. The chronicler Walsingham loads him with responsibility for the *bal des Ardents* 1392, a disaster in which Charles VI was almost incinerated during a masque.

An even more venomous enemy of Henry's was Waleran of Luxembourg, Count of St. Pol, who had four years before been present at the proposed Trial by Battle between Henry when Duke of Hereford and Mowbray, the Duke of Norfolk. The Count of St. Pol had married Richard II's half-sister, Princess Joan's daughter by her first marriage to Sir Thomas Holland. Professing himself anxious to avenge Richard's death, the Count threatened in a letter written on February 10th 1402[11] "by every means in my power...I will do you every mischief by sea and land beyond the limits of the kingdom of France." During 1403 (December) St. Pol committed many acts of piracy in the English Channel, attacking the Isle of Wight where he captured some poor fishermen. St. Pol obviously resented Richard's betrayal by his cousin and Henry's cousin, Edward Duke of Aumerle, for he had a figure of Aumerle made to represent him when Earl of Rutland in his Castle of Bohain and carried to the gates of Calais.[12] A gibbet was then erected and a figure hung on it by the feet representing the Earl of Rutland. It was cut down by the English garrison.

Henry IV appointed his younger son, the Lord Thomas, lieutenant in Ireland during 1401. He was only a boy, a year or so younger than the Prince of Wales, but he and Thomas Cranley, Archbishop of Dublin and Chancellor of Ireland, were soon embarrassed by financial difficulties, like Hotspur and Prince Henry in Wales. Cranley was obliged to write to Thomas of Lancaster's father a letter heavy with complaints. "Your son is so destitute of money that he has not a penny in the world, nor can borrow a single penny, because all his jewels and his plate...are spent and sunk in wages."[13] Because of lack of wages his soldiers were leaving his service, and members of his household were on the point of retiring from his service.

Thomas of Lancaster wrote to his father from Drogheda on February 18th 1402 sending Master Stephen Le Scrope "to plead before you concerning the charge of your Castle of Roxburgh."[14] (Le Scrope was its warden.) Shakespeare in *Henry IV* alludes to Thomas being Prince Henry's favourite brother. There is no evidence of this, but Thomas was later to be envious of his brother's fame as a soldier and tried hard to emulate him. He stayed two years in Ireland.

To strengthen his shaky position as king, Henry was anxious to promote dynastic marriages for his daughters. When his elder daughter Blanche (no doubt named after Henry's mother) married a German Prince Louis of Bavaria, the son of Rupert Duke of Bavaria, the King anxiously wrote to the Treasurer to be provided with money for Blanche's journey to Germany during the summer (1402). His council suggested a suitable means would be the King's "Collectors of our Customs and subsidiaries of wool, hides and wooly skins of many parts of our kingdom."[15] Negotiations were also begun about this time for the marriage of Henry's younger daughter Philippa to King Eric of Denmark and Sweden, but the marriage did not take place until 1406.

Meanwhile the relentless and ferocious war with Wales continued. Henry's contemporaries such as Archbishop Arundel, considered that the King was humane and forgiving to his enemies and Hoccleve, the poet, depicted him as a king with a merciful heart, though he often had great cause for vengeance.

Among Henry's bitter enemies were the Franciscan friars in Wales, many of whom believed the stories that Richard was still alive. One captured friar from Aylesbury boldly confronted the King. Henry questioned him:

"What would you do if Richard did come forward again?"
"I would fight for him though I had nothing but a stick in my hand," replied the man.
"And what would you have done with me" demanded the King.
"I would have you Duke of Lancaster."

The King had him beheaded.[16]

Adam of Usk related how Llewellyn ap Griffith Vaughan of Cayo in the county of Cardigan, a man of gentle birth known for his liberality, being well disposed to Owain, was brought before Henry IV and the Prince of Wales during the autumn (1402). By the King's command he was hanged, beheaded and quartered. Owain and his men also indulged in many atrocities, cruelly hanging the lordship of Ruthyn in North Wales and ravaging the countryside with fire and sword, and carrying away the spoils of the land and the cattle to the mountains of Snowdonia.

Adam never admitted the reason for his exile by the King, owing to his dishonesty in stealing some sheep, which forced him to travel to Rome and elsewhere (February 19th, 1401-1402). He relates the hardships of the journey, how after passing Lucerne and its wonderful lake, he "was drawn in an ox-waggon half dead with cold and with mine eyes blindfold lest I should see the dangers of the Pass (Mont St. Gotthard) on the eve of Palm Sunday (March 18th)." For the medieval traveller there was the terror of an awesome comet, seeming to predict the death of the Duke of Milan. He was to remain in exile until 1411, in disgrace with Henry IV, but he then secured a pardon.

Events in Wales still favoured Owain, for in early February 1402 by a cunning ruse he succeeded in capturing Grey, whose few troops had been surrounded, then overpowered in the Welsh passes by superior numbers. Deserted by his own followers, the Marcher Lord was removed to the mountains of Caernarvon where he became Glyn Dŵr's close prisoner for eight months. His capture was an awful setback for his friend King Henry, who together with his Council and Parliament were determined to allow Grey to purchase his freedom. Eventually he agreed to pay 10,000 marks (about £6,000) to his captors to be handed over before St. Martin's day (November 11th). He was later freed, a ruined man.

The Brut Chronicle is incorrect when it alleges that Owain made Lord Grey wed one of his daughters. Surely *The Brut* is confusing Grey with Sir Edmund Mortimer, younger brother of Roger, Earl of Mortimer, killed at Kells in Ireland and uncle of the boy Edmund, the rightful heir to the throne by the strict laws of heredity, detained by the King at Windsor.

Sir Edmund Mortimer had been born in Ludlow during November 1376 and at the very moment of his birth people said that the horses in his father's stables were found standing up to their knees in blood, an evil omen. Yet a brilliant future for Edmund was predicted by the Welsh seers which was not to be fulfilled. When Owain revolted against the English in 1400, Mortimer acted in concert with his brother-in-law Harry Percy in resisting the rebellion. However, Henry IV mistrusted Mortimer, perhaps out of fear, knowing that Sir Edmund's nephew's claim to the throne was a more valid one than his own.

On June 22nd 1402 one of the most able of Owain's captains, Rhys Gettin, met a strong army marching from Ludlow under Sir

Edmund Mortimer at Pilleth in Wales, not far from Knighton in Herefordshire, and after a bloody battle the Welshmen were triumphant. In his mention of the fight Adam's sympathies were divided, because Edmund Mortimer's father Earl of March and Lord of Usk, had been his early esteemed patron. Edmund, the most powerful of the Marcher Lords, was captured and held prisoner by Glyn Dŵr in the Welsh mountains, and many of his Welsh tenants are said to have deserted to Owain. King Henry now suspected that Mortimer was no reluctant prisoner. Glyn Dŵr treated him kindly, ready to acknowledge Edmund or his nephew as a possible King of England. Rather cleverly, to wean him completely from Henry, the Welsh rebel arranged that he should marry one of his daughters, Katherine. Mortimer was disgusted at the King's refusal to ransom him. Meanwhile Henry, during October, seized Mortimer's plate and jewels, depositing them in the Treasury. Hotspur made every effort to persuade Henry to ransom his brother-in-law, as he had ransomed Lord Grey, but the King turned a deaf ear to his pleading. It was Henry's stubborn refusal to do anything, that was ultimately to turn Hotspur into a rebel.

Too little is known about the Lady Elizabeth Percy, Hotspur's wife (Shakespeare's Kate Percy), but it is probable that she was a more determined character than we encounter in *Henry IV*. She was born at Usk in Monmouthshire in 1371, the elder daughter of Edmund Mortimer, the Earl of March by his wife Philippa, daughter and heiress of Lionel Duke of Clarence, Edward III's third son, so she had royal blood in her veins. Dugdale merely relates that her father bequeathed her and Harry Percy in his will a salt cellar in the form of a dog, a little cup made like the body of a harp, with the head of an eagle. Hotspur did not need his wife to spur his ambition, as there is evidence during the Battle of Shrewsbury (1403) that he aspired to be king.

Henry IV had many enemies. The Franciscan friars continued to travel all over England and Wales organizing conspiracy and spreading untrue rumours that King Richard was still alive.

The King, now aged thirty-six, had been a widower for eight years when he was married by proxy on April 3 1402 to Joanna of Navarre, the widow of Duke John IV of Brittany. On the elderly

Duke's death during November 1402, she had become Regent for her son. Her father was Charles the Bad, King of Navarre. It seems very likely that Henry and Joanna had met earlier, perhaps at his cousin Richard's court, when the Duke and Duchess of Brittany had visited England. Henry was attracted to her, for aged thirty-three she was handsome, and in her maturity had acquired grace. Certainly Henry was in haste to marry her. At the proxy marriage service, at Eltham, Joanna's envoy Anthony Ricz, represented her.[17] There is a letter from Joanna to her future husband written in Vannes during February 1400 in which she writes that she is desirous to hear of his good estate.[18] This letter was to be delivered in England by a lady named Joan de Bavalen.

Agnes Strickland relates that she was the first widow since the Norman Conquest to be crowned Queen of England.[19] Henry's half-brother, Henry Beaufort, Bishop of Lincoln, officiated at the marriage ceremony in Winchester Cathedral. The expenses amounted to £433.6s.8d. King Henry's gift to his bride was a collar purchased from a London jeweller for 500 marks (£333.6s.8d), while his two younger sons, Prince John of Lancaster and Prince Humphrey presented their stepmother with a pair of tablets from a London goldsmith costing £79.[20] Joanna's coronation in Westminster Abbey took place (February 26th 1403) and a contemporary manuscript[21] depicts her as a majestic and graceful woman. After the ceremony a splendid tournament was held in which Beauchamp, Earl of Warwick "kept joust on the Queen's part against all other comers, and so notably and knightly behaved himself, as redounded to his noble fame and perpetual worship."

Despite her rectitude and suitability as the King's Consort, Joanna was never popular in England, mainly because the English disliked foreigners. Parliament readily, during 1404, deprived her of various foreign members of her household, no doubt wishing to make much needed economies. Henry, however, was a generous husband, granting his Queen 10,000 marks per annum to be paid by the Exchequer, until he could give her lands of that value. It amounted to a further burden for the royal purse. The marriage gained the King very little political or other advantage.

The Bretons descended on the south-west coast and burnt Plymouth. Henry hoped to make an alliance with Brittany, but piracy continued on the high seas, and the cost of Queen Joanna's household preyed on his mind, On her part the Queen was forced to leave her large family in Brittany, not a light sacrifice for such a devoted mother. Henry, uxorious by temperament, was always faithful to Joanna and we do not hear of any discord.

For Henry's elder daughter Blanche's marriage, the King on the advice of his Council resorted to an aid. An aid was a feudal custom, fixed by the Statute of Westminster (1257). It usually consisted of 20s on a knight's fee and on each £20 worth of land.[22] Henry also had to borrow from John Hende, a rich London merchant, and others. More than £16,000 was raised during the summer (1402). Blanche met her bridegroom, Louis of Bavaria, and Count Palatine of the Rhine - son of Rupert III of Bohemia and lately elected King of the Romans - in Cologne in late June and they were married at Heidelberg on July 6th. In the negotiations, the King had promised to give his daughter a dower of 40,000 nobles, but he encountered difficulties in obtaining the money and the final payment of 5,000 nobles was not made until 1444, during the reign of his grandson Henry VI.[23] Blanche was only thirteen at the time of her happy marriage, but she died four years later in May 1406.

1402 was a deeply troubled year for King Henry, and during May, the Black Prince's illegitimate son, known as Sir Roger de Clarendon, engaged in a desperate conspiracy against the King, together with several Franciscan friars, the prior of Launde in Leicester and others. We know nothing about Roger's mother, except that her name was Edith de Willesford, and he was probably born at the royal palace of Clarendon (Wiltshire) before the Black Prince's love marriage to Princess Joan of Kent, mother of Richard II. In his will the Black Prince left Sir Roger de Clarendon a silk bed. Both Edward III and Richard II treated Roger generously, for the old king granted him an annuity for life, while Richard confirmed it, creating him a Knight of the King's chamber. However, in the summer of 1398, Sir Roger was rash enough to wound Sir William Drayton in a duel, and the knight subsequently died from his wounds. After being indicted for murder, Roger absconded and for several years remained a fugitive at large, to be regarded as an outlaw.

His involvement in a plot against Henry IV was to cost him his life, for on May 19th he was arrested by the Mayor of London and taken to the Tower, where he was charged with treason.[24] Both Roger and the Franciscans had spread rumours that his half-brother Richard II was still alive. They were found guilty, to be drawn on hurdles to Tyburn, where they were cruelly treated and hung. Another accusation was of sending money to Glyn Dŵr in Wales. Three years later in 1405, Roger's execution was to be included among the alleged crimes committed by Henry IV, compiled by Richard Scrope, Archbishop of York, in a manifesto. This was one of the most serious rebellions against Henry, instigated by the Earl of Northumberland and Scrope, one of the Archbishops who had crowned him in October 1399.

VI   The Percy Rebellion

The ravaging and plunder of England and Scotland continued during the early summer (1402), despite the temporary truce. On May 7th, Hotspur and his father, commanding strong forces, inflicted a crushing defeat at Nesbitt Moor on the Scots, who had invaded Northumbria. Their commander Patrick Hepburn of the Hales, was taken prisoner by the Percys. Holinshed, the sixteenth century chronicler, relates that Archibald 4th Earl of Douglas, son of James, killed at Otterburn (1388), was "more displeased in his mind for this overthrow", and wanting to avenge it, invaded the border country with over twelve thousand men during the following August. The usual scenes of desolation followed; the plunder of farms and the burning of the crops of the terrified peasants as the Scots advanced through Northumberland and Durham. However, returning homeward with their booty, they were intercepted on the morning of September 14th by Harry Percy, the Earl of Northumberland and George Dunbar, the Scottish Earl of March, now Henry IV's ally and an excellent military strategist.

The English troops occupied a commanding position at Millfield-on-Till in the borderland of the Cheviots, about six miles north of the market town of Wooler, while the Scots halted at Homildon. The site of the battle is Akeld Bastle. In his impetuous way, Harry Percy was eager to charge the enemy at the head of his army, but was dissuaded by George Dunbar. He urged that the superb English and Welsh archers should open the attack by a continuous discharge of arrows. The archers, expertly trained, formed and reformed their ranks, discharging their arrows with deadly precision, throwing the enemy into utter confusion. The valiant Archibald Douglas, despite wearing a suit of armour of exquisite workmanship, was pierced with six wounds. Falling from his horse, he was taken prisoner by Hotspur himself, while hundreds of his men fell dead or wounded on the battlefield. A story is told of a brave knight named Sir David Swinton crying to his compatriots: "What fascinates you today that you stand like deer or fawns in a park to be shot, instead of meeting your foes hand to hand. Descend with me to conquer, or fall like men." As one hundred men followed Swinton down the hill, they were met by the deadly onslaught of arrows. No armour, lance or helmet could withstand it. Others, including 500 Scots, were drowned in the Tweed, trying to escape from the Northumbrians. The men-at-arms played little part in the English victory. Besides Douglas, the Earls of Fife, Angus, Moray, and Orkney, and many knights were taken prisoner, to be lodged in the castles of Greystoke, Dunstanburgh and Roxburgh. Thirty French knights were found to be allies of the Scots.

The news of the Percy victory made a great stir in London, and Hotspur's esquire, Nicholas Sherbury, a Northumbrian, who brought the intelligence to Henry IV, was rewarded with an annuity of £40, confirmed by Parliament on September 25th. However, to the consternation of the Earl of Northumberland and his son, peremptory orders arrived from Henry to the Percys in Alnwick Castle that none of the prisoners were to be ransomed or liberated under any pretext whatsoever. This was an ill-advised action by Henry, though probably dictated by his insolvency rather than envy for the mighty achievement of the Percys which was in marked contrast to the King's failure in Wales.

For their part, father and son regarded the King's action as a breach of chivalry and a provocative insult. Northumberland, Henry's 'Mathias', was justified in making a dignified protest, a matter of honour. By immemorial custom "they who had undergone the danger of battle should have all the advantage of pay and prisoners." The kings of England had always allowed this right "to the lords of the north, to encourage them in defending their dominion, and to keep up the damages by the continual depredations of these faithless people the Scots." Adam of Usk, in exile abroad, believed that the victory of Homildon Hill made the House of Percy "too much puffed up",[1] inciting them to become rebels a year later.

On Friday October 20th, Northumberland, now aged sixty, brought before the King and the assembled Parliament in Westminster, six of the principal prisoners captured at Homildon. They included young Murdoch Stewart, son of the Duke of Albany, Sir Adam Forster, Lord Montgomery, Sir William Grahame, two French knights and an esquire. As they entered the hall, the proud captives had to kneel several times before the King, who stood in front of the throne. Henry spoke coldly to their spokesman Sir Adam Forster, blaming him for not honouring his promises, but he always warmly praised courage, even in his enemies, and he told Murdoch Stewart that he had nothing to fear, having been captured fighting like a brave soldier. Later the prisoners were entertained at the King's table in the painted chamber.

Henry raged because Archibald Douglas was not among the prisoners, and a heated argument took place between Northumberland and the King. As for the Percys, they were dissatisfied with the money allowed them by Henry. Always outspoken, the Earl urged him for payment for the custody of the Marches. Reproachfully he said: "My son and I have spent our all in your service." Henry answered abruptly: "I have no money and money you shall not have." The Earl said: "When you entered the kingdom you promised to rule according to our counsel: you have now year by year received large sums from the country, and yet you have nought, and pay nought...God grant you better counsel." There was no sign yet that he intended rebellion. However, his growing jealousy of Ralph Neville, Earl of Westmoreland, the King's brother-in-law and intimate friend gnawed like a poisoned cancer in his breast. Neville's second wife was Joan Beaufort, Henry's half-sister. He continued to show Westmoreland increasing favour.

When Henry IV's fourth Parliament assembled at Westminster on September 30th, it petitioned the King to render Northumberland some special honour and reward for his victory over the Scots at Homildon. The nobleman's popularity had surged hugely. When Henry granted to the Earl the whole of the Scottish estates of the Earl of Douglas, Northumberland heard of it with a wry smile, for he would receive no financial benefit whatsoever, unless the lands of Douglas were conquered.

Hotspur continued to turn a deaf ear to Henry's demand for Douglas to be brought to London without delay. Whether there had ever been a staunch friendship between Henry and Harry

Percy, unlike his father, is open to doubt. The King was well aware that Elizabeth, Hotspur's wife, was Sir Edmund Mortimer's sister. Her nephew was also named Edmund Mortimer. She was the mother of two children, Henry now aged eight, born at Alnwick Castle (February 3rd 1394) and Elizabeth later to marry John, Lord Clifford. He now suspected Hotspur of intriguing with Owain Glyn Dŵr and conspiring with Sir Edmund Mortimer.

According to *The Brut Chronicle*[2] a tense and highly dramatic interview took place between the King and Harry Hotspur during the autumn (1402). When Percy entered the royal presence, Henry asked him, "Where is the Earl Douglas? Have you brought him with you?" Hotspur accused Henry of not allowing his brother-in-law to ransom himself with his own money as Lord Grey had done. Then the King became very heated, exclaiming that public money must not be used outside the country to help his enemies (the Welsh). Hotspur retorted, lapsing into a stammer, characteristic of him when angry: "How is this? You would have us expose ourselves when you and your crown is in danger, and yet you will not help us?" *The Brut Chronicle* says:[3] "Anon after, fell a debate betweene the Kyng and Sir Henry Percy, that was called amonge the Scottes Henry Hotespurre. This Syre Henry came unto the Kyng, and asket of hym certeyn wages that he was behynde, for the kepyng and wardeynship of the Marches, and the Kyng hym gave but a light answare." When the King "sore aggrevid", struck Hotspur's cheek, Percy retorted "by my faith this shal be the derrest-boght buffet that ever was in England." Thereupon, turning his back on Henry, he took his horse and galloped back to northern parts with his men, who had accompanied him to London. Apparently Henry soon repented of the estrangement between them, for he sent for Sir Harry again, but he refused to come to court.

There is some evidence that Henry was surprised by the Percy rebellion in July 1403,[4] but in view of his deteriorating relations with the Percys, can this be true? Why did he make a point of antagonizing them in insisting that none of the prisoners were to be ransomed after the battle of Homildon? The Earl had surrendered his prisoners, but Hotspur had categorically refused. Was Henry jealous of their achievements? On March 3rd 1403 he granted to the Earl of Northumberland a great part of southern Scotland, comprising the estates of the captive Archibald Earl of Douglas, probably a gesture of reconciliation on Henry's part. The most satisfying explanation for the rebellion is that the Percys were deeply dissatisfied with Henry as king, and wanted to control the crown. Henry IV suspected that the Percys themselves had designs on the throne, as he declared on the eve of the Battle of Shrewsbury, according to the chronicle of *Dieulacres*.

When people descried a star in the firmament known as "Stella Comata" they shook their heads, for they were very superstitious. They thought it signified evil auguries.

Hotspur made a firm ally of Archibald Douglas whilst holding him as prisoner, and later acquired his invaluable aid at the Battle of Shrewsbury.

Prince Henry appointed Lieutenant of Wales in 1403, was obliged to write to the Council that he needed money for the payment of his troops and for relieving and provisioning the garrisons of Harlech and Aberystwyth Castles, besieged by the Welsh.[5] Reporting to the Council he wrote that he had burnt Owain's houses at Sycharth and Glyndyfrdwry. At Shrewsbury he was in such acute need of money that he was compelled to sell his jewels.[6] His father, on arriving at Higham Ferrers, and on hearing of his son's plight wrote to the Council during July, asking them to pay the Prince £1,000 on behalf of his troops. He, himself, proposed to continue his journey to Scotland to help the Percys in their border warfare.

Meanwhile Henry's devoted servant Hugh de Waterton, in poor health, wrote to his master disturbing news from Wales, that Owain and his men had lately set fire to the towns of Llandilo and Newtown[7] and that the Chamberlain of Carmarthen had been driven out and his men killed. On July 6th the castle and town of Carmarthen surrendered to the Welsh after a short siege. However, their leader suffered a reverse in Pembrokeshire when Thomas Lord of Carew routed the Welsh.

Many of the conspirators plotting against Henry IV were superstitious, believing in the prophecies of Merlin, the Welsh Arthurian seer. These prophecies, chanted by the bards in the mountains of Snowdonia and repeated in the shires across the

English border, stated that King Henry was the Moldwarpe cursed of God's own mouth, and the Glyn Dŵr, the Percys and Mortimer were the dragon, the lion and the wolf, who would divide the realm between them. These vain prophecies were later scoffed at by the historian Holinshed, dismissing them as foolish credit, but he never understood what a firm hold they had on the minds of the people.

King Henry first learnt the gravity of the Percy rebellion at Burton-on-Trent, July 15th. Faced with a crisis, Henry was always at his best, making the bold decision to march with his army from Lichfield to Shrewsbury, a matter of sixty miles, thus cleverly anticipating Hotspur's movements. George Dunbar urged on Henry the necessity of striking before the rebels could consolidate their forces. Above all, it was essential to cut off their army before they could unite with Glyn Dŵr near Shrewsbury, or effect a juncture with Northumberland's forces in the north. When later Hotspur saw the royal standard floating over Shrewsbury, he was dumbfounded, realizing that he had been outwitted by Henry, for he would have preferred to have been the first to secure the town. Hotspur had made the fatal mistake of underestimating Henry.

Among Hotspur's most devoted followers were the men of Cheshire, superb archers, and many of the people still revered Richard II's memory, even believing that he was still alive. On the night of July 9th, Harry Percy stayed at the house of Petronilla Clark in Chester, whose son John Kyngesley was among his most devoted friends. Meanwhile Hotspur's uncle, the Earl of Worcester, sometime Governor of the Prince of Wales and Steward of the Royal Household, had deserted Henry IV and joined his nephew in the north. Leading Cheshire families such as the Leghs, Beestons, Vernons and Winningtons, were proud to serve under Hotspur's standard, displaying the white hart, Richard II's badge.

Among Harry Percy's many accusations against Henry IV in his proclamation, together with his father Northumberland and uncle Worcester was "that thou modest an othe upon the Holy Gospelles bodely touched and kissed by thee at Doncaster, that thou woldest never claim the Crowne, Kyngdome or state royall, but onely thyne owne propre inheritance and the inheritance of thy wife in England." As Henry's first wife had died in 1394, it is not evident what they meant. Their accusation of procuring Richard's death by foul means rings rather hollow as Northumberland is supposed to have been among the peers urging Henry to have his cousin killed. Henry was also charged with perjury that he had exacted taxes from the clergy and the people without the consent of Parliament. Henry's treatment of Sir Edmund Mortimer still rankled with Hotspur, for Henry of Lancaster had falsely accused Mortimer of willingly yielding himself a prisoner to Owain Glyn Dŵr, though he had been cast into prison "and laden with iron fetters, for thy matter and cause and neither wouldest thou deliver him thyself, nor suffer us, hys kinsmen, to ransom and deliver hym." The Percys called themselves the true defenders of the Commonwealth in their manifesto.

The Battle of Shrewsbury fought on Saturday July 21st 1403, was one of the most decisive in medieval history, determining the dynasty that was to reign in England for the next sixty years. The Prince of Wales was vastly relieved when his father's army probably outnumbering the rebel troops, entered Shrewsbury, for his men, dangerously exposed and even isolated, had been recently raiding North Wales.

Hotspur, perforce, unable to gain access to Shrewsbury, withdrew his troops, perhaps numbering 14,000[8] men, along the Whitchurch road for about three miles and a half, occupying a carefully chosen site on the slope of Hayteley Field. In front of Harry Percy's men were fields already ripening with crops of peas and vetches. Hotspur's lodging for the night, together with his uncle the Earl of Worcester, was in the small village of Berwick, lying on the banks of the Severn. He was a prey to anxiety, for the morning of July 21st dawned ominously with no news of the whereabouts of his ally, Owain Glyn Dŵr. Scouts were in vain sent across the Severn. The probable reason for Owain's absence from the field of Shrewsbury was that he, too, had been taken aback by the rapidity of Henry's movements in advancing on Shrewsbury. He himself maintained that he had been delayed by floods in Carmarthenshire. Various reasons were offered for Owain's tardiness; his alleged mistrust of the Percys and the fear of betrayal, the charge that he did not like open pitched battles, preferring skirmishes, guerrilla fighting and furtive raids, but none of these reasons seems plausible. Owain was a leader of meritorious courage and had everything to gain by King Henry's defeat. The legend that Glyn Dŵr watched the battle from the top of an oak at Shelton, one and a half miles from Shrewsbury, is without foundation.

Harry Percy's father's absence from Shrewsbury was another misfortune for the rebels, since his reinforcements might well have turned the tide of battle. Hardyng, Hotspur's faithful squire, attending on Percy throughout the battle, is very scathing about Northumberland, accusing him bitterly of having sacrificed his son and "faylled hym foule withouten will or rede." However, it is probable that the old nobleman was genuinely ill. While on his way southward he had to be carried in a litter near Tadcastle at the head of large forces. Shakespeare in the mouth of Rumour in *Henry IV, Part 2*, refers to old Northumberland lying "crafty-sick" in Warkworth Castle, "this worm-eaten hold of ragged stone." In reality the Earl retired from Tadcastle to Newcastle. Both Holinshed and Daniel mention Northumberland's illness, but do not attribute it to craft. When Worcester laments his brother's absence, Harry Percy is more sanguine, saying:

> It lends a lustre and more great opinion,
> A larger dare to our great enterprise,
> Than if the Earl were here...[9]

Northumberland may well, of course, have thought his eldest son too rash in precipitating the rebellion.

Hotspur made such a hurried departure from the house of a family name Betton at Berwick that he forgot his favourite sword. The two armies faced each other on the terrain now known as Battlefield. It was customary in medieval times for priests to be used as intermediaries, and Henry sincere in his attempts to avoid what he knew would be a bloody battle, sent Thomas Prestbury, Abbot of Shrewsbury, with a message to Hotspur and Worcester, inviting them to visit the royal lines to discuss their grievances. Most contemporary chroniclers relate that Hotspur was somewhat moved, and decided to send his uncle Worcester to negotiate with the King.

Most of the contemporary chroniclers such as John Capgrave (he was aged ten in 1403) and a later one, Ralph Holinshed, are hostile to Worcester, blaming him for the breakdown in negotiations. He was not to be trusted. Yet earlier in his career he had been much esteemed by John of Gaunt as a fine soldier, and foreign sovereigns had considered him a statesman of high honour whose word was his bond. There was a heated conversation between King Henry and Worcester. He told the King that he ruled worse than King Richard. According to Capgrave, he told Henry "Thou spoilst yearly the relme with taxes and tallages, thou paest no man, thou hedist no laws, thou art not the heir of the relme." The King hotly retorted: "I take tallages (taxes) for nedis of the relme, and I am chosen Kyng be comone (common) assent of the relme, wherefore I counsel the to put the in my grace." Worcester replied: "I trust not thi grace" and realizing that further discussion availed nothing, Henry said, "Now I may pray God that thou must answer for alle the bloode that here shalle be shed this day and not I."

Capgrave does not mince his words. "But that Architophel the Earl Thomas (Worcester) pretending to be a mediator between Henry Percy and Henry IV but false to both, was alas, the cause of all the ruin, the cause of al the sorrow." Holinshed described the Lord Thomas Percy as one "whose studie was ever (as some write) to procure malice and put things in a broil." Shakespeare, following Holinshed, makes Ralph Neville, Earl of Westmoreland, say to the King when referring to the prisoners Harry Percy refuses to surrender after Homildon:

> This is his uncle's teaching. This is Worcester
> Malevolent to you in all aspects.[10]

Holinshed is at least correct when he describes Henry IV's reign as one of "great perplexitie and little pleasure." The contemporary chronicler Giles considered both Henry and Hotspur equally culpable, while the *Dieulacres* chronicler, a Cheshire monk, accuses Henry of joining battle, though fairly enough he offered the rebels every concession.

When Hotspur ordered his esquire to equip him with his favourite sword he had used at Homildon and many a battle, he replied: "Alack my Lord. It was left behind at the place where you encamped overnight, the village of Berwick." Hotspur shuddered, chilled by sudden memories, exclaiming: "Now I see that my ploughshare is drawing to its last furrow, for a soothsayer once told me in my own country that I should perish at Berwick. Alas!

he deceived me by that name, which I believed to mean Berwick in the north." He remembered that a comet that had appeared in early 1403 could be seen in the sky. Hotspur shared most of the superstition, so prevalent in that age. Shakespeare's Hotspur is a magnificent character, but the real man is unlikely to have taunted Owain Glyn Dŵr for his faith in the dreamer Merlin, nor his prophecies.

Once again George Dunbar, the Scottish Earl of March, was at Henry's side, urging him to attack quickly, for a speedy victory was essential lest Percy's father in the north or Owain in Wales came to his assistance. Perhaps it was George Dunbar, who advised Henry that two of his household knights should be dressed in the royal surcoat, a cunning ruse that deceived Hotspur and his ally, Archibald Earl of Douglas. However, Henry was no craven coward. His worst enemy could not deny his bravery as a soldier.

Hotspur, usually over-confident, seemed a little downcast, perhaps depressed by the misadventure at Berwick when he addressed his men. They would have followed him to Hell. He might have been Edward, the Black Prince, at Poitiers when he told his troops, "It is better to fall on the battlefield, in the cause of the common weal, than after the battle to die by the sentence of the enemy."

Henry IV's army, more numerous than Percy's, was drawn up in three divisions. The main body commanded by the King was on the right, while the Prince of Wales with his division was on the left, and in the centre the Earl of Stafford. As Sir Charles Oman remarked, this was the first battle in which two English armies fought each other with the long-bow,[11] though the long-bow had often been used against the crossbow and men-at-arms.

The trumpets rang in the still summer air as a cruel and bitter battle began at midday, the like of which had never been seen before in England. The cries of the two opposing armies could be heard, "Esperance, Percy", while Henry's men responded, "Saint George upon them." Hotspur's Cheshire archers, some of them wearing their Ricardian white hart badges, were in the front, and when the King's archers came within range they were greeted by fierce fire. They retaliated with some success, but the aim of

Hotspur's archers was so accurate that Henry's men were forced to break ranks and plunge down hill. Taking advantage of their plight, Percy sent his men-at-arms in pursuit. Some of Henry's men fled the field.

Percy's preliminary success did not last for long. Far from retreating the Prince of Wales's division had managed to consolidate its position. Now advancing against the enemy, they managed to drive back Hotspur's right wing and by their skill get to the rear of the rebel troops, while they were concentrating on fighting the King's division.

Early in the battle Prince Henry was wounded in the face by an arrow - a painful wound, but he bravely refused to retire from the field. As Henry said, "If the Prince runs, who will stay to end the battle". Holinshed wrote: "The Prince that daie holpe his father like a lustie young gentleman." He relates that the Prince never ceased, either to fight where the battle was most hot or to encourage his men. Holinshed does not mention the Prince saving his father's life when fiercely attacked by Archibald Douglas as Shakespeare does.

It was a cruel internecine fight to the death. While the battle was yet undecided, Harry Percy and Douglas, with the object of slaying the King himself, followed by thirty chosen knights, forced their way through the medley of confusion, to the accompaniment of the groans of the wounded. How expertly did Douglas wield his great battle-axe, striking at those unfortunate enough to obstruct his way. How terrible were the sufferings of wounded soldiers! Sir Walter Blount, a brave knight, dressed in the surcoat of the King, was killed, as was the Earl of Stafford, who commanded the vanguard. Holinshed wrote that Douglas, thoroughly frustrated, said: "I marvell to see so many kings thus suddenlie arise, one in the necke of another." And Shakespeare, more dramatically makes him say, "Another King! they grow like Hydra's heads." The King fought bravely, killing many a knight with his own hand, but the Scottish George Dunbar, Earl of March, sensing Henry's great danger, persuaded him to retire to the rear.

The battle was at its height and its outcome still uncertain when Hotspur, sweating and gasping for air, unfortunately raised his vizor, to be struck by an arrow from an unknown combatant, which pierced his brain. Just before his men had exultantly cried "Henry Percy, King", but they were rejoicing too soon. Perhaps he had hoped to see Glyn Dŵr's troops cross the Severn and fall on Henry's rear. The shouts now turned to "Henry Percy, slain." With the loss of their gallant leader, the rebels were put to flight. According to Holinshed, "the earle of Douglas for hast, falling from the crag of an hie mounteine, brake one of his cullions" and was taken prisoner; so was the Earl of Worcester, sorely grieving for his nephew Hotspur, Sir Richard Vernon, the Baron of Kinderton and many others suffering the same fate. Holinshed gives the losses of the King's army as sixteen hundred killed, and four thousand grievously wounded. The casualties of the rebel Percy were about five thousand. The poet Daniel wrote:

> Such wrecke of others blood thou didst behold
> O furious Hotspur, ere thou lost thine owne!
> Which now once lost that heate in thine waxt cold,
> And soone became thy armie overthrowne,
> And O that this great spirit, this courage bold,
> Had in some good cause bene rightly showne!

All his contemporaries emphasized Hotspur's rashness.

The battle had lasted three hours.

Night fell and darkness descended on the stricken battle-ground. The eclipse of the moon, from half-past eight until almost midnight, cast its eerie influence, intensifying the horror. All around could be heard the faint groans of the wounded and cries of pain as the strippers or so-called "pilours" prowled among the bodies of men-at-arms, archers and knights, royalists and rebels alike. They despatched the wounded and robbed the dead of any valuables they might possess. It is related that Henry searched the battlefield for Hotspur's body and that he could not refrain from tears when he found him. At first he allowed Harry Percy's kinsman, Thomas Neville, Lord Furnival, to remove the body from Shrewsbury and to inter him for one night in his family chapel at Whitchurch. Then anxious that everybody might be certain that he was dead, he ordered his body to be exhumed and exhibited "bound upright between two millstones." In Shrewsbury marketplace by the pillory lay the remains of the charismatic rebel, so loved and admired during his thirty-seven years, a macabre experience for many to gaze at. Lest anybody might believe that Hotspur was still alive, Henry had his head smitten off and set up at York, an act denounced by Richard Scrope, Archbishop of York, for its cruelty. Harry Percy had presented such a menace to Henry's throne that King Henry's real purpose was to prevent people believing in his survival.

As for Thomas Percy, Earl of Worcester, when he saw his nephew lying lifeless, he shed tears, declaring that he no longer cared for any evil fortune in store for him. He was beheaded two days later with Sir Richard Vernon and his head set up on London Bridge. Wylie relates that Henry vowed to erect a hospice on behalf of the souls of the slain. Six years later a chapel was endowed and a daily mass sung for those who had fallen in the battle. All is silence now. The church is dedicated to St. Mary Magdalene and is known as Battlefield even today.

Hotspur's fellow-conspirator Archibald Douglas, was eventually ransomed in 1408, but continued to raid the English border from 1412-22.[12] Fighting with the army of Charles VII against the infant Henry VI of England, he was killed at Verneuil (1424). He was nicknamed Tyeman (the loser), but was probably fortunate to have survived so long.

In his chronicle, Enguerrand de Monstrelet gives the wrong date for the Battle of Shrewsbury. He praises the courage of the King, slaying with his own hand thirty-six men-at-arms. It was Lord Thomas Percy, not Hotspur taken prisoner and executed after the battle.[13]

As for the Lady Elizabeth Percy, Henry no doubt suspicious of Sir Edmund Mortimer's sister, had first had her arrested, to be soon released. She had her Harry's remains buried many years later in the Northumberland tomb in York Minster. She was later married to Thomas Lord Camoys, described as a henchman of Henry IV, though formerly a favourite of his cousin Richard. In 1401, Camoys was summoned to take part in the Welsh war against Owain Glyn Dŵr. Elizabeth's second husband served bravely at Agincourt (1413) under Henry V. She predeceased Camoys, dying during April 1417 and is buried in a resplendent tomb in the Church of St. George at Trotton, near Midhurst in

West Sussex. There Hotspur's Welsh widow lies beside her second husband, dressed in an attractive kirtle and mantel with her Mortimer arms on the Camoys tomb.

The defeat of the Percys presented the Earl of Westmoreland with a further opportunity to show his loyalty to King Henry, and to destroy the power of his great rival in the north, the Earl of Northumberland. After meeting Westmoreland and Robert Waterton south of Newcastle-on-Tyne, Northumberland withdrew there, but the burgesses would only admit the nobleman with a few servants and refused to accept his troops. He then retired to Warkworth Castle, that lovely home of the Percys, set high above the gentle River Coquet, so medieval with its ancient 14th century bridge and church of St. Lawrence. Westmoreland sent urgent messages to the King suggesting he should send siege engines, so as to capture Northumberland's castles of Alnwick and Warkworth. On August 11th the old nobleman was coldly received by Henry. Northumberland surrendered to him. Wylie states that he excused himself from any participation in the rebellion, blaming his eldest son and declaring that Harry Percy had acted without his authority. However, the Earl acknowledged that he had offended. He was compelled to give up Warkworth, Alnwick, Berwick, Cockermouth and Prudhoe (on the Tyne) to royal commissioners, while the King bestowed the office of Constable of England on his third son, John of Lancaster, a boy of fourteen. Hardyng tells us that the Earl was briefly imprisoned at Bagyngton near Coventry.

The custodian of the Percy strongholds in the north, loyal to the Earl, refused to transfer their allegiance without remonstrance. For instance, Sir William Clifford refused to surrender Berwick Castle unless Hotspur's son Henry was restored to the rights and dignities now pertaining to him as Northumberland's heir.

One thing is clear, the former friendship between the King and Earl was no more. Northumberland might dissemble, but a burning resentment against Henry IV gnawed at his heart. Northumberland, however, was restored to his estates six months later.

According to Wylie, before Henry left York, he was boldly accosted by a soothsayer, whose reputation was high, for he had foretold Richard II's downfall. He now reproached Henry, who in no mood to be thus censured, harshly ordered his head struck off.

Having subdued the rebellion in the north, the King had once again to turn his mind to Wales. The situation was extremely dangerous. On September 3rd 1403, Richard Kingeston, Archdeacon of Hereford, and now Dean of Windsor (he had formerly served Henry when Earl of Derby as Treasurer for war in Prussia and elsewhere), was writing a desperate letter to the King from Hereford, where the Welsh were enjoying considerable success. He begged Henry to come in person to Wales. "War'for, for Goddesake, he wrote, thinketh on zour' beste Frende, God, and thanke hym as He hath deserved to zome; and loveth nought that ze ne come for no man that may counsaille zoew the contrarie; for, by the trouthe (truth) that I schal be to zowe zet, this day the Welshmen supposer and truster that ze schulle nought come there, and therefore, for Goddesluve, make them fals men...[14]

Henry did not get further than Worcester at this time, because he had not sufficient money or supplies for an expedition. At Worcester the lords had to renew their oaths of allegiance to the King. Meanwhile the Constable of Kidwelly Castle, one of West Wales's finest, with its great gateway, was writing to Henry that all the rebels of South Wales, aided by men from France and Bretagne, were advancing towards the Castle of Kidwelly "with all their array and there have destroyed all the grain belonging to your poor lieges..." He feared unless there was speedy succour the castle would be destroyed and all the garrison undone.[15]

Thomas Pennant in his *Tour in Wales* opines[16] that Owain's great oversight was to neglect to attack Henry's forces immediately after the Battle of Shrewsbury when they were tired and vulnerable.

VII   Henry's Crowning Error

After the death of John of Gaunt, his third wife, Katherine Swynford, Duchess of Lancaster, had gone to live in Lincoln, where she enjoyed an annual allowance of 1000 marks granted her by her stepson Henry IV from the revenues of the Duchy of Lancaster.[1] She was a generous benefactor to Lincoln Cathedral, giving the authorities chasubles of red velvet and bowdekins, orphreys of gold leopards among other valuables. Wylie dubs her rather uncharitably "infamous adulteress", but she was in fact a most remarkable woman. She died on May 10th 1403, to be given a magnificent funeral in the Angel Choir. There she lies in the chantry erected to commemorate her, and at her feet lies Joan Beaufort, her daughter by John of Gaunt, Countess of Westmoreland, and grandmother of two future kings.[2] Our present Queen Elizabeth II is descended from Henry VII's mother, Lady Margaret Beaufort, from John Earl of Somerset, the eldest Beaufort son. There is no means of knowing whether Henry IV felt any particular emotion when Katherine died.

Perhaps the most remarkable of Katherine's sons was Henry Beaufort, Bishop of Lincoln (1398), and Bishop of Winchester (1401), and Henry IV's Chancellor for two years from 1403-05. A proud and ambitious man, he possessed great ability. He became the tutor of the young Prince of Wales, and he was more intimate with him than King Henry. In Henry Beaufort's early life he had an illegitimate daughter Joan by Alice, daughter of the Earl of Arundel.[3] This partly explains Archbishop Arundel's dislike of Beaufort, seducing his brother's daughter. Later he became the leader of a political faction directly opposed to Archbishop Arundel and the King, favoured by the Prince of Wales.

At the Parliament summoned to meet at Westminster on January 11th 1404, Bishop Beaufort of Lincoln played a prominent part, explaining to the members that King Henry needed their

110

advice and counsel to deal with such pressing matters as the recent rebellion of the Percys, now suppressed, the rebellion in Wales, the raid on the Isle of Wight by the Count of St. Pol, the troubles in Calais and Guyenne and the hostility of Louis, Duke of Orléans.[4] Sir Arnold Savage, known for his verbosity, was again appointed Speaker, though he accepted the post reluctantly, knowing that he had been too free with his criticism of the government. Lord Rees of Hanlake was Treasurer. This Parliament met in the refectory of Westminster Abbey each morning at eight o'clock.

On February 6th, Northumberland's case was heard by the Lords and Commons. They now decided that the Earl, always a favourite, had been guilty of a trespass against the King's authority, rather than treason. Consequently he was fined and restored to some of his honours and dignities, though no longer High Constable, and stripped of his possessions in the Isle of Man. Northumberland continued to plot secretly against Henry IV.

George Dunbar, the Scottish Earl of March, received rich rewards from King Henry for his services at Shrewsbury, large grants of land, including the Earl of Worcester's house in Bishopsgate. George Dunbar was always eager to claim relationship with Henry, but there exists correspondence possibly written in August 1404 and later, between the Scottish Earl of March and his wife Christine to Henry, complaining of their financial difficulties causing them hardship. Christine blames the hostility of the followers and friends of the deceased Sir Henry Percy preventing her and her husband from retiring to their fortress Colbrandespath.[5] The pestilence was raging, making matters worse.

Henry was certainly far more amenable to Parliament's wishes than Richard II. For this he deserves some praise. When they asked him to remove four persons from his household, the Abbot of Dore, the King's Confessor, Master Richard Derham and others, he acquiesced, though he knew of no reason for their removal.

He was, however, becoming increasingly unpopular, partly because of his lack of success in Wales and partly because the presence of Queen Joanna and her Court increased the expenses of the royal household, arousing all the insular prejudices of the

English. When the King perfectly reasonably asked Parliament for money for defence, the members retorted that Henry already possessed all the revenues of the Crown, and of the Duchy of Lancaster, as well as the profits of various forfeited lands and wardships. However, Archbishop Arundel was active in his negotiations with the Lords and Commons. It was arranged that twenty shillings should be taken from each knight's fee, and one shilling from each pound's worth of land or goods.

The Parliament of early January (1404) lasted for sixty-seven days, but accomplished little. As soon as the session terminated, Henry and his Court moved restlessly about to Eltham for Easter, then to Windsor and eventually to Pontefract, where the Earl of Northumberland visited the Court with his three grandsons during late June.

Henry possessed one excellent quality as a king to be commended. He was diligent, as it was essential for him to be on amicable terms with monarchs overseas, who acknowledged that he was King of England. Among *The Royal and Historical Letters* there is an interesting letter from John I, King of Portugal, written in Portuguese, referring to their mutual alliance with the King of Castile.[6] John I was Henry's brother-in-law, having earlier married Philippa, elder daughter of John of Gaunt. It is evident that Henry adhered to this alliance. Earlier on September 9th 1403, at Worcester, he had commanded all the admirals of his kingdom to give free passage to the King of Portugal's ambassador, Johannes da Silva, about to return to Portugal.

At least in his official correspondence Henry IV is conciliatory enough, promising to make restitution of various goods, which were a matter of dispute between England and Spain.

In 1404 most of the chronicles, including *The Brut* and *Adam of Usk* mention how Henry IV continued to be troubled by devoted servants of the former King Richard II. William Serle, for instance: "Yeomen of King Richard's Robys 'come yn to England out of Scotland, and said to divers people that King Richard was alyve yn Scotland', and so, moch of the people beleved his wordez; wherefore mych of the peple of the relme were yn gret erroure and gruching (grumbling) ayens (against) the King." At last he was taken prisoner on the northern border by Sir William Clifford and brought to Henry while he was in Pontefract. Serle was alleged to be the murderer of his uncle the Duke of Gloucester, so much detested by Richard II. According to Wylie, he was finally executed (at Tyburn) with more than ordinary cruelty, suffering "more and severer penalties than other of our traitors have endured before these times."[7]

The war continued in Wales. The Prince of Wales, eventually far more successful than his father, in 1404 was faced with great difficulties. As his lieutenants, the shifty Duke of York served him well in South Wales and the Earl of Arundel in North Wales.

During this year Harlech Castle, surely the most sublime of the great Edward I's castles in Wales, built between 1283-1289, in its wonderful position commanding a superb view of the sea, fell into Owain Glyn Dŵr's hands.[8] It is situated in Merionethshire, twenty miles from Dolgellaü; its architect a man of genius, James of St. George.

From October 1403 it was strongly suspected that some of the garrison sympathized with the rebels and were mutinous, especially the Constable, William Hunt, who was indeed preparing to surrender the castle to the Welsh. After being seized by soldiers of the garrison, he was kept a close prisoner in the castle for three months. However, Hunt with two yeomen named "Jack" Mercer and Harry Baker entered into secret treaty with the rebels and they were whisked away. The small garrison of five Englishmen and sixteen Welsh held out desperately, led by a heroic Englishman, Vivian Collier, finally to fall into Owain's hands. The capture of Harlech and Aberystwyth Castles gave Owain unfettered authority in Central Wales, for Harlech became the residence of his Court and family. There is a tradition that either at Machynlleth, Harlech, or at Dolgellaü, Owain was formally crowned as Prince of Wales and envoys were present from Scotland, France and Spain. At Machynlleth - and there is no place more Welsh in spirit - Owain summoned a parliament of his supporters and one can today visit a Hall of State where this parliament was held. A parliament was also held at Harlech. During a later siege during the Wars of the Roses, Harlech Castle was held by the Lancastrians, and tradition relates that the patriotic song *Men of Harlech* was then composed.

Aberystwyth and Cardigan Castles under the command of Sir Thomas Burton, had garrisons of twelve men-at-arms and forty-five archers.[9] Far too small one would have thought to make the castles secure. Burton was forced to yield these castles to Owain before January 12th 1405. Criccieth Castle in its superb position overlooking Tremadog Bay, fell into Owain's hands in 1404, to be fatally sacked and burnt. The garrisons of the castles of Conway, Flint and Beaumaris on the Isle of Anglesey, were too scanty, and the wages of the garrisons were much in arrears. Beaumaris (beautiful marsh), the last and largest of the castles in Wales to be begun by Edward I in 1295, was captured by the Welsh in 1404; it was not recovered until 1405. In the town a medieval house (32 Castle Street), now an antique shop, dates from 1413.

Charles VI of France never accepted the change of dynasty in England and a formal alliance was forged between Wales and France in 1404. Owain cleverly reminded the French that his ancestor Sir Owain of Wales had fought gallantly, shedding his blood for France during the Hundred Years' War against Edward III. When negotiating with the Welsh, Owain referred to himself, "Owynus, dei gratia Princeps Walliae", a challenge to the English Prince of Wales. The French agreed never to sign a separate peace or truce with Henry IV. French support was conditional on Owain acknowledging Benedict XIII, Charles VI's candidate as Pope, in Avignon. His letter to the King of France shows his shrewdness as a diplomat:

Most Serene Prince,

You have deemed it worthy on the humble recommendation sent to learn how my nation for many years now elapsed had been oppressed by the fury of the Barbarous Saxons...But now, most serene prince, you have in many ways, from your innate goodness informed me and my subjects very clearly and graciously concerning the recognition of the true Vicar of Christ...

Owain cleverly makes his recognition of Benedict conditional on France agreeing to recognize the Bishopric of St. David's as independent from Canterbury.

Among those who deserted the cause of King Henry during 1404 for that of Owain Glyn Dŵr was John Trevor, a Welshman who had been created Bishop of St. Asaph in 1395. He was immediately deprived of his bishopric but remained a loyal follower of Owain even in adversity.[10] With his experience, Trevor was very useful to Owain, travelling to France to seek the aid of armed men. A French expedition under the Count de la Marche consisting of five hundred armed horsemen and two hundred crossbowmen, assembled in the English Channel but never reached the west coast. This proposed invasion is referred to in a letter written in Latin by the Bishop of Bangor to Henry IV.[11]

During 1404 Owain and his French allies invaded Herefordshire, advancing as far as Woodbury Hill, eight miles from Worcester. There they were confronted by Henry's army and made to withdraw. Once again, however, the capricious elements proved the Welsh rebels' best ally. When the King's army during September besieged Coety Castle in Glamorganshire, violent storms and flooding of the rivers of Glamorgan forced him to retreat. Owain succeeded in capturing forty wagons of Henry's baggage train, containing jewels and other valuables. The royal army was compelled to retreat to its base in Hereford. Owain retired to the Welsh mountains, unwilling to seek a pitched battle.

Glyn Dŵr was a magnificent leader, full of fire and magnetism, a man of remarkable determination and courage. He possessed many of the qualities of a statesman, imaginative and bold, holding no narrow vision of eventual victory and the course to pursue later. Even the French and the Scots were impressed. Owain's rebellion raised a terrible conflict of loyalties for many leading Welsh families, torn for several generations between their allegiance to the King or a Marcher lord (English gentry with estates in the marches or borders of Wales) and often tempted to turn to Owain. Later, after 1406 when the English seemed to be gaining the upper hand, many supporters of Owain deserted to Henry, among them William Griffith, a member of the Tudor family who first founded the fortunes of the Tudors, and Penrhyn Castle. Among those most hostile to Owain were burgesses of the boroughs in Wales, who collaborated with the Marcher lords. Some Welsh people, for example David Gam of south-east Wales, ancestor of the Herbert family, was bitterly opposed to Owain. Families were sometimes divided, brother against brother; Robert, Abbot of Barnsey, supported the rebels, while his brother Evan ap

Meredith suffered for his firm adherence to the cause of Henry IV. Not only were his houses burnt, but he was killed defending Caernarvon Castle against the rebels.

One problem that gave the King considerable anxiety was trade with the German and north European cities, known as the Hanse. Baltic trade was vital both for England and for Prussia and the Hanseatic towns. The English exported wool or cloth made from it, while the Hanse supplied fish, chiefly herring and dried cod, for English appetites, furs, timber for shipbuilding and other essential products. Friction, however, often occurred in which the order of Teutonic Knights was concerned, for they had become rulers of large parts of Prussia and the Baltic lands.[12] Their Grand Master was elected for life by the Knights. Both countries suffered damage and inconvenience when ships were detained and goods seized, leading to considerable resentment when the Grand Master arrived in England during the summer of 1403 to claim damages for over £6,000. The complaints by the aldermen of the Hanse to Henry that their ships were being seized and that the merchants of Hamburg were sustaining losses owing to the misbehaviour of English sailors can be studied in *Royal and Historical Letters*.[13] Henry himself wrote to Conrad de Junginger, the Grand Master, a letter in Latin concerning the dangerous state of the high seas owing to the depredations of pirates and promising to provide remedies. It was a matter for the second Parliament of 1404 meeting at Coventry in October when it was decided to send an embassy to the Baltic. This Parliament is chiefly notable because its members did not include lawyers, so it was called "the unlearned parliament". It was considered that they devoted too much time to their clients' interests, instead of attending to the King's business. The Commons appointed as their speaker Sir William Sturmy, the member of Parliament for Devon. Bitter attacks were made on the Church, deeply distressing to Archbishop Arundel.

The early fifteenth century was seldom free from plots. Young Edmund, Earl of March and his brother Roger, great-grandsons of Lionel, Duke of Clarence, whose claim to the throne was superior to Henry IV's, were being kept in strict confinement at Windsor. Their guardian was Constance, Lady Despenser, wanton by nature, sister of the Duke of York. Henry thought that

116

they were absolutely secure, but Lady Constance managed to free them in the middle of February 1406, having procured false keys. Fleeing towards South Wales, hoping to join Glyn Dŵr, who might proclaim Edmund as King of England, they were captured near Cheltenham and brought back to King Henry, who had started in pursuit of them. Brought before the Council in London, Lady Despenser not only accused her brother Edward, Duke of York of plotting their escape, but also planning to murder the King at Eltham Palace during the previous Christmas. York was arrested and imprisoned for a few months in the Tower, to be released. When he was not involved in conspiracies, York gave Henry IV good service in Gascony and serving in the Council. The worst fate fell to the wretched Smith, who had made the false keys. His hands were chopped off, according to Holinshed, followed by his execution.

Henry IV's wanton sister Elizabeth, the former wife of the Duke of Exeter, Richard II's half-brother, had married as her third husband Sir John Cornewaille. Henry behaved generously to his sister, granting them 1,000 marks yearly for life and later various other grants. Sir John Cornewaille excelled at jousting, which probably endeared him to King Henry. A son was born to Elizabeth and her husband in the middle of February 1403, and Henry acted as godfather. She seems to have lived happily with Cornewaille, surviving until the reign of Henry's grandson Henry VI.[14]

Among those involved in the plot to abduct the Earl of March and his brother was Thomas Mowbray, named the Earl Marshal, now aged nineteen, son of the late Duke of Norfolk, who had died in exile. Mowbray confessed that he knew of the plot, but was pardoned. It is obvious, however, that he was badly disposed towards the King. Even Archbishop Arundel was suspected of complicity in the conspiracy to free March, but was cleared.

A far more dangerous rebellion was to break out on May 28th (1405). The Earl of Northumberland had never been sincere in feigning friendship with King Henry. After Berwick Castle and Jedburgh Castle had been restored to him during the previous November, Northumberland remained in close touch with Owain Glyn Dŵr and Sir Edmund Mortimer. During February (1405) the celebrated Triple Convention, whose purpose was to partition England, was signed in the house of the Archdeacon of Bangor in North Wales. It was proposed that Northumberland should have England north of the Trent, the counties of Warwickshire, Northamptonshire, Leicestershire and Norfolk. Owain was to take not only Wales, but all lands west of the Severn and south of the Mersey, while Mortimer was to have all southern England.

Using poetic licence, Shakespeare in a famous scene at Bangor makes the historic event, the Triple Convention, occur at least eighteen months before the battle of Shrewsbury. Always fascinated by the Percys, there is the brilliant characterization of Hotspur, and simultaneously he brings the great Welsh rebel Glyn Dŵr vividly to life with some memorable passages showing his mystical sense of destiny:

> At my nativity
> The front of heaven was full of fiery shapes,
> Of burning cressets, and at my birth
> The frame and huge foundation of the earth
> Shak'd like a coward.[15]

There are those lovely lines, like wanton music, where Owain when referring to his Welsh daughter, Lady Mortimer, married to Sir Edmund, his son-in-law, says:

> She bids you on the wanton rushes
> lay you down,
> And rest your gentle head upon her lap,
> And she will sing the song that
> pleaseth you,
> And on your eyelids crown the god of sleep.[16]

The chroniclers Giles and Holinshed both mention the Tripartite Convention.

The brains of the rebellion of 1405 was Richard Scrope, Archbishop of York, who had once been sent by Richard II on an embassy to the Pope in an attempt to get Edward II canonized. He came of an illustrious family, the Scropes of Masham, mostly doughty soldiers. The Archbishop of York was closely connected by marriage with the Percys of Northumberland since his younger brother John had married the widow of the Earl of Northumberland's younger son Thomas, and his sister Isobel was the wife of Sir Robert Plumpton, a rich tenant of Northumberland's near Spofforth Castle, also involved in the rebellion. Richard Scrope was on the friendliest terms with the Percys, and although he had supported Richard II's deposition six years ago, was now hostile to Henry IV. The Percys were munificent benefactors of York Minster.

Scrope may have been responsible for drafting and approving the manifestos against King Henry, which were being publicized and posted on the doors of churches in York. There were ten articles, mostly reflecting the accusations of Hotspur two years earlier. Possibly it was the work of a number of proctors.

Henry IV was an usurper, who had broken his oath and falsely dethroned Richard II.[17] He had promised to abolish levies of fifteenths and tenths and the subsidies and customs on wool and wine, but had also broken his promise here. Although Scrope had crowned Henry, together with the Archbishop of Canterbury, he now alleged that Henry had made a false claim to the crown and had connived at Richard II's murder. Not only had he procured the deaths of the rebel Earls, but also the deaths of Roger of Clarendon, the Black Prince's illegitimate son, and Sir Henry Percy (Hotspur). He had confirmed statutes directed against the Pope and the universities, and brought misery on the country. The manifesto asked for help to put the lawful heir on the throne, but the provision was deliberately vague.

Not only was Northumberland heavily involved in this rebellion, but also his great friend Thomas, Lord Bardolf of Wormegay, in the Marchland near Lynn, Norfolk. A nobleman now aged thirty-seven, he had been born in 1368 at the manor of Birling near Cuckmere Haven in Sussex. A giant of a man, a brave soldier like Northumberland, but possessing little political intelligence. He was also connected by family interest with the Earl of Northumberland, and animated by a violent hatred of Henry IV. Another supporter of the Earl's was Thomas Mowbray, son of Henry's former enemy, the Duke of Norfolk, who had died in exile in Venice.

When he was at Hereford on May 23rd, King Henry received sudden news of this fresh rebellion, and always at his best in a crisis threatening his throne, acted with decision. Returning to Worcester, at the head of his army, he was in Derby by May 28th, where he wrote to the Council. Then he moved rapidly northward. By June 3rd he arrived at Pontefract.

Ralph Neville, Earl of Westmoreland, always loyal to Henry IV, probably from self-interest and the desire to profit from the disloyalty of his rival, the Earl of Northumberland, advanced towards York, together with Prince John of Lancaster, Henry's third son, a boy of fourteen. Westmoreland, inclined to be treacherous and cunning by nature, was eager to pay off old scores against Northumberland, but his troops were few. The chronicler John Stow, writing much later in the sixteenth century, relates that the Archbishop of York's power was far greater than Westmoreland's. Clad in armour, Archbishop Scrope was a venerable figure, exhorting his army consisting not only of citizens of York, but of knights, gentlemen and yeomen coming from neighbouring farms. The Archbishop was much loved for his amiability and esteemed for his integrity and incomparable learning. He now promised his followers forgiveness of sins "to all them whose hap was to die in the quarrell".[18] The two opposing armies faced each other at Shipton Moor, about six miles from the city of York. All around lay the forest of Galtree, dark and menacing.

Westmoreland now subtly asked the Archbishop "for what cause" (contrary to the King's peace) his followers had come in armour. The Archbishop replied that he wanted peace, not war. He and his company had taken up arms "for feare of the King to whom he could have no free access" because there were a multitude of flatterers about Henry. Messengers passed to and fro between the two parties. After further parley Westmoreland promised to redress their grievances and suggested to Richard Scrope that he should disband his army. The Archbishop, too trustful of Westmoreland, persuaded his followers, nothing loath, to go to their homes, although the Earl Marshall, Thomas Mowbray, tried to dissuade him.

While the lords were drinking together "in loving fashion", Westmoreland was secretly increasing his forces. Quite unexpectedly he arrested Richard Scrope and Mowbray and others. Westmoreland, by a despicable ruse had got them in his power. They were accused of high treason and brought as prisoners to Pontefract, where Henry IV had arrived, from thenceforth to be taken back to York.

The King's act of having Archbishop Scrope condemned and beheaded was his worst mistake, for which he suffered remorse for the rest of his life. Both contemporary chroniclers and later historians find it hard to explain, for the execution of Scrope amounted to judicial murder. Henry has been justly criticized. The murder of Becket in Canterbury Cathedral by four unauthorized, emotional assassins in 1170, a crime, vile enough, was perhaps less dreadful than the crime of beheading another Prince of the Church. Twenty-four years earlier Simon Sudley, Archbishop of Canterbury, had been seized by a bestial rabble during mass in the Tower of London and beheaded on Tower Green, another vile crime.

In allowing the Archbishop of York, who had crowned him together with the Archbishop of Canterbury, to undergo a humiliating death, Henry cast away every scruple, giving way to evil passions. Was Henry vindictive by nature? In his earlier life, when he usurped his cousin's throne, he had sometimes exercised mercy, but now he was taking part in a gross injustice.[19] An interesting precedent had occurred seventeen years ago when Richard II's friend Alexander Neville, Archbishop of York, had been declared guilty of treason. Parliament had hesitated on this occasion to take his life. Instead he was banished the realm and died in exile.

Henry IV's Lord Chief Justice in 1405 was Sir William Gascoigne, born about 1350 according to Wylie.[20] As a member of Gray's Inn he had studied law. The buildings were so cramped that aspiring lawyers "had to lodge double, or sleep two in a bed." It was usual for a judge in the fifteenth century to have first served as a Sergeant-at-law. Rising to eminence before 1391, during the reign of Richard, Gascoigne was created a Sergeant-at-law and retained on the Council of Henry when Earl of Derby.

When the King summoned Sir William to his presence, he fearlessly refused to take part in the trial of an archbishop, or to sentence him to death for taking up arms against the King. *The Giles Chronicle* mentions the Christian name of Gascoigne incorrectly as Johannes.

Henry had no difficulty in finding an obsequious member of his Court Sir William Fulthorpe, to preside at a trial, misnamed for it undoubtedly was a travesty of justice. Gascoigne knew his precedents and the Canon law, and that an archbishop could not be sentenced by a secular court.

Archbishop Arundel, a predecessor of Scrope's at York, had been on friendly terms with the churchman ever since being appointed Bishop of Ely[21] when Scrope served under him, though they later had political differences. He now set out in a desperate attempt to save his friend's life, riding all day and through the night on Whit Sunday to intercede on his behalf with the King. When Henry saw him at Bishopthorpe on the Monday, he urged Arundel to rest after his tiring journey, probably an excuse for not taking his advice.

Meanwhile a court consisting of the Earl of Arundel, the Archbishop's nephew, Sir Thomas Beaufort, eldest of the Beaufort brothers, and Sir William Fulthorpe condemned Scrope to death and the Earl Marshal Mowbray and Sir William Plumpton as traitors to be beheaded.

One strong reason for Scrope's rebellion was his increasing discontent with Henry's and Parliament's policy towards the church. He feared, not without reason, that the King in his desperate need for money might adopt a scheme for secularization of ecclesiastical funds.

Archbishop Scrope remained resigned to his fate, for he said manfully and serenely, "I shall die for the laws and good rule of England", and was hurried to his execution in early June, together with Mowbray, in a field of barley near York. Dressed in a scarlet chynes or riding cloak with a violet hood over his shoulders, the King's creatures bent on humiliating him, set him "on a sorry nag not worth a nail". The executioner took five strokes to sever his head. *The Brut* says, "Anon, God of his grete godenesse wroust (wrought) and shewyd meny grete myracles for his worthi clerke, the Archbishop of York, that was dorn to deth." The rebellious people, deeply shocked, deemed him a saint, for he was indeed a martyr.

It was now that the King was smitten with a mysterious and terrible illness, divine justice people thought, for the execution of Archbishop Scrope. *The Brut* said that the King was a victim of leprosy, but this seems extremely unlikely. He continued to mix freely with people. Whatever the illness, Henry's health never really recovered and he was often an invalid for the rest of his life. Whilst at Ripon, two eye-witnesses were horrified when they saw great pustules appear on his face and hands. 1405 was a critical, disastrous year in his life, for he emerged from it a shattered, unhappy man. Wylie wrote that the King was disturbed at Ripon by a hideous dream, so that he cried out in agony that he was on fire. The Northern folk declared among themselves that it was the voice of God giving a dire warning that he would be struck down with leprosy as a punishment for the death of the martyred Scrope.

John Capgrave, the contemporary chronicler, alleged that "the King after that tyme lost the beaute of his face. For as the comonne opinion went, fro that tyme until his deth he was a lepir and evyr fowlere and fowlere." For a handsome, athletic man such as Henry, very attractive to women in his younger days, it must have been a devastating experience to be thus smitten. Medical opinion has differed about the Kings illness. It has been diagnosed as acute erysipelas and a form of gangrenous ergotism contracted from diseased rye during Henry's Prussian campaign in 1390, when Earl of Derby. Some have suspected syphilis, but as already mentioned Henry, whatever his faults, was chaste by nature and there is no evidence that he was unfaithful to his first wife, Mary de Bohun, whilst overseas.

To the people of York, Richard Scrope became a saint. So many people visited his tomb in the Cathedral fenced about with a parclose of wood, that Prince John of Lancaster ordered the sub-treasurer to have the fence removed and to prevent the mass of "false fools" to resort there to make their devotions.[22] Henry IV had his own candidate as the new Archbishop of York, a former protégé of John of Gaunt's, but another candidate, Master Robert Hallum, was favoured by Pope Innocent VII.[23] If it had not been for the papal schism, the King would have been excommunicated.

King Henry was by now deeply unpopular, not only in northern England but throughout the country, blamed for his failure in Wales and elsewhere, though successful in retaining his throne. His cousin Richard, always fond of display, had in 1395 - ten years previously - attended the York plays and pageants in this beautiful medieval city, near the gates of Trinity Priory, close to

Mickle-Gate bar. For Henry, however, constantly on the move to put down rebellion, such diversions could not be indulged in.

The Earl of Northumberland and Lord Bardolf managed to escape into Scotland, where they sought asylum with a loyal friend, Sir David Fleming, who was acting as guardian to the old man's grandson, Hotspur's son Henry.

By the beginning of July, the King was at Warkworth, after capturing Prudhoe, another Percy stronghold. When besieging Warkworth Castle, Henry IV brought with him not only cumbrous stone-casting catapults, but newly invented guns. He was almost as interested in artillery as Alfonso d'Este, Lucrezia Borgia's third husband, in the beginning of the sixteenth century. One of Henry's guns was so powerful that no walls, however strong, could withstand the missiles it hurled. Warkworth's intrepid custodian John de Middleham, made a stout resistance. It was not until the seventh discharge of artillery and a shot from an enormous piece of ordnance that shattered one of the towers, that the garrison was forced into submission. Warkworth became the headquarters of Prince John, appointed by his father Lord Warden of the East Marches.

Alnwick Castle was the last of the Percy strongholds to be besieged by the King, where the garrison commanded by Sir Henry Percy of Athol (another of the Earl's grandsons) stoutly held out until Berwick Castle had yielded.[23] The garrison of Alnwick were allowed to move out with all the honours of war. By July 14th King Henry was installed in the Castle. He had been successful in quelling the rebellion, but Northumberland and Bardolf had eluded him for the present. They were declared traitors in Parliament.

VIII   Henry Gains the Upper Hand

It was at Grosmont, then a border village situated in the valley of the Monnow in Wales, that Owain Glyn Dŵr sustained his first serious defeat. The Welsh troops were under the command of Owain's best commander, Rhys Gethin, who had inflicted a crashing defeat three years earlier at Pilleth on Sir Edmund Mortimer. In early 1405, Rhys with 8,000 men passed through Glamorgan and after skirting Abergavenny, attacked Grosmont on March 11th 1405 and partly burnt it. Grosmont Castle, the birthplace of Henry IV's grandfather Henry of Grosmont, was under the command of Sir John Skidmore, representing the King's friend Hugh Waterton. Young Gilbert Talbot[1] was a gallant and talented soldier, much esteemed by the Prince of Wales, and he and the small English garrison succeeded in defeating the Welsh, who fled panic-stricken, leaving from 800-1,000 dead on the field.

The Prince of Wales, now aged eighteen, already an experienced soldier, wrote an account of the battle to his father from Hereford, praising the bravery of Gilbert, Lord Talbot, his brother John and the other commanders leading the men against superior numbers. He wrote: "Yet it is known that victory is not in the multitude of the people but in the power of God and well was this shown." If in 1403-1405, Prince Henry grew to maturity as a commander in the field, it was in the latter part of his father's reign that he learned the art of supreme military command.[2]

During May at Pwll Melyn near Usk, the English gained another victory, killing 1,500 Welshmen and taking many prisoners, including Owain's son Graffydd, who was sent to the Tower.[3] His brother Tudor was killed in the battle. The war was now going badly for the Welsh rebels, particularly when the Chancellor, Dr. Graffydd Young, was captured a few weeks later. It was Young and a relation of his wife, John Hanmer, who had handled the negotiations between Owain and the King of France.

During August, French troops under the command of Marshal Jean de Rieux, consisting of 800 men-at-arms, 600 crossbowmen and 1,200 light horse, after disembarking at Milford Haven, joined a Welsh force and marched into England within eight miles of Worcester, where the King was campaigning. They thought it prudent to withdraw rather than to fight, alarmed at Henry's strength.

The Parliament meeting in early March 1406 in Westminster, and not at Coventry or Gloucester as at first proposed, an important one, was the longest of Henry IV's reign, lasting from March 1st until December 22nd. Thomas Langley, soon to become Bishop of Durham, was the new Chancellor, while Sir John Tiptoft, who had been in the service of the King for some years when Earl of Derby, was appointed Speaker. He proved as outspoken as Sir Arnold Savage, not afraid of acting independently if need be. Earlier he had probably shared Derby's exile in France during 1398, returning with him to England when he deposed Richard and was rewarded with various grants, including the apparel of the attainted Thomas Mowbray, Duke of Norfolk. When appointed Speaker, he was evidently a young man, for he made the usual pleas that he should be excused service on account of his youth and lack of experience. The King did not quarrel with John Tiptoft, but he soon tired of the Speaker's ever recurring mention of the grievances of the Commons. For instance, Henry was too free in the bestowal of grants, having the effect of reducing his revenue. The Commons were determined to resist demands for taxation.[4]

Tiptoft was well disposed towards the Prince of Wales, requesting in Parliament that Prince Henry should remain continuously in Wales to wage war against the rebels. He sought an assurance that lands recovered from them should not be granted to anybody for at least three months. He suggested that the Prince of Wales should be thanked by letters under the Privy Seal for his invaluable services in Wales. Parliament insisted in a move hostile to the Queen Consort that all aliens, both Bretons and French, should be banished from the kingdom. In the early fifteenth century their duties were to represent the grievances of the people, while the role of the Lords was rather to give counsel.[5] Before the end of this Parliament, Tiptoft became a Councillor and Treasurer of the royal household.

James, the second son of Robert III of Scotland, was a romantic character. His elder brother David had died mysteriously in 1406. To preserve James's life, it was proposed that the young prince should be sent to France to be educated, but off Flamborough Head he was waylaid by an English ship at the end of March and languished long years of imprisonment under the Lancastrian kings. Henry said jokingly he would have him educated and so he was. When Robert III died in 1406, James succeeded his father as James I of Scotland. Actually because of the temporary truce between England and Scotland, James's capture was illegal. His nature was artistic, for he became not only a skilled musician, but a fine poet in the Chaucerian tradition. His love of music would have appealed to Henry IV. Later he fell ardently in love with Joan Beaufort, daughter of John Beaufort, Earl of Somerset, eldest son of John of Gaunt and Katherine Swynford. He married her in St. Mary Overy (now Southwark Cathedral) in 1424 just before his release from captivity. He told the story of his love for her in his poem *The Kingis Quair*.[6]

A letter in an interesting collection of *Royal and Illustrious Ladies* throws a curious light on the occasional refractory behaviour of nuns at the beginning of the fifteenth century.[7] On November 12th 1400, the Prioress of Rowney, a Benedictine nunnery in Hertfordshire, wrote to King Henry complaining that Sister Joanna Adelsbey, a nun of this Order, "wanders and roams abroad from country to country, in a secular habit, despising her vow of obedience, to the grievous danger of her soul, and manifest scandal of her order." She begs Henry to use his power for the capture of Joanna, so that she could be chastised according to the rule of her order. We do not know what happened to the nun.

Henry's half-sister Joanna Beaufort, now the Countess of Westmoreland, not to be confused with the daughter of John Beaufort, Earl of Somerset, was on friendly terms with the King and during 1406 wrote to him on behalf of an esquire named Christopher Standith and his wife Margaret, whose father Thomas Fleming had formerly been in the service of John of Gaunt. Christopher Standith had given King Henry devoted service in

Wales and on his travels, but he and his wife with their many children were now somewhat impoverished. Her letter[8] shows her in a favourable light, for she entreats her half-brother to find a suitable place for them in the household of Henry's Queen Joanna.

Henry IV remained all his life on affectionate terms with his sister Philippa, Queen of Portugal (since 1387) - he had once given her a wine-flagon in 1382. She made John I of Portugal an admirable queen, even tolerating his bastards and treating them kindly. She persuaded the young Earl of Arundel to marry Beatrix, one of John's natural daughters, though he did so reluctantly, wishing to marry the girl of his choice, an unusual license in the early fifteenth century. Prior to his marriage he had promised a large sum of gold to King Henry to allow him to choose his own wife. After his marriage to his Portuguese bride, he was astonished by the King's demand for the promised money, seemingly a very mercenary act on Henry's part. In this dilemma Arundel turned to Queen Philippa. She wrote tactfully to her brother on November 4th 1405 from Lisbon, "And since you know well, my supremely best-loved brother, that he is now married not after his own seeking, but as by your commandment in part of my instance, I therefore supplicate you since you are so great and noble a prince...that it will please you to quit claim to the said sum at this my request, in order that I, who am in part the cause of his marriage, may be the cause of the acquittal of the said sum.[9]

The King again suffered ill health during 1406, being afflicted by the mysterious malady that first devoured him at Ripon. When Henry and his court travelled from Eltham to Greenwich during Easter, he was unable to ride from Eltham to Windsor to attend the feast of St. George. It was less exhausting for him to go by barge. Wylie wrote that Henry was a delicate man. The constant burden of kingship, the hardships of his campaigns in Wales, and the remorse he suffered for the execution of Archbishop Scrope, all exacted their toll. In Henry's household expenses, moreover, there are constant references to physic. As a young man of twenty he had been twice ill during 1388, afflicted with the "pokkes", signifying some eruption on the skin, especially on the face, called "measles". In 1390 he paid 6d to a barber for blood-letting and on his first expedition to Prussia with the German Knights, he was so prostrated with illness at Königsberg that the Grand Master's physician had to be summoned from Marienburg to attend him. In 1403 his surgeon John Bradmore provided £2 for medicines, hardly an abnormal payment for a royal patient. One thing is clear: Henry IV's doctors, including Master Malvern, were baffled by the symptoms, so that his advisers had recourse to an Italian doctor, David di Nigarelli of Lucca in Tuscany, known to the English as Nigarill. He stayed on in England as a naturalized subject and was evidently highly esteemed by the King, being created Warden of the Mint and given a salary of 80 marks (£53.6s.8d). Some time in 1412 Nigarelli further benefited, being granted the manor of North Stawndon in Wiltshire. Henry obviously appreciated the services of his Italian physicians, since Pietro de Aldobasse, appointed in 1410, was beneficed with prebends such as the Deanery, Wimborne Minster. Whether the foreign doctors were more successful in diagnosing Henry's malady is not known. It is no exaggeration to dub him a neurotic in his later years.

He was temporarily well enough to travel to Lynn on July 18th 1406 accompanied by his queen and the Prince of Wales, Thomas and Humphrey, to take leave of his younger daughter Philippa, who was fifteen and about to marry Eric XIII King of Denmark, then aged twenty-four. It was a dynastic marriage, wisely conceived by King Henry to strengthen England's links with Scandinavia. John Capgrave was only a small boy at the time, but he remembers Philippa in the town of Lynn as "she went on board the ship in which she left England." Their wedding took place at Lund.

Philippa's escort was impressive, including Bishop Bowet of Bath and Wells, to be created Archbishop of York in 1407, Henry, Lord Scrope of Masham, a kinsman of the ill-fated Archbishop and a brilliant, cultivated aristocrat, Sir Henry Fitzhugh and others. Capgrave was present on another historic occasion when the King's grandson Henry VI laid the foundation stone of the College of Eton in 1440. He survived until 1464 when he died at King's Lynn during the reign of Edward IV, aged 70. According to the chronicler, men of literary eminence told him that Henry IV was a man of great ability and that they enjoyed their intercourse with him. He stresses his amazing memory, but to compare him to Solomon is too flattering, for he lacked much of his wisdom.

Henry's studious nature can most readily be perceived during his rare periods of leisure or rest. After he left Lynn he continued his journey to Spalding in Lincolnshire, then to Horncastle and on to Bardney Abbey to be received by the Abbot John Woxbrigg and his monks. After hearing two masses in St. Mary's Chapel, Henry had breakfast with his two sons Thomas and Humphrey in the Abbot's room.[10] This King was a strange mixture, so guilt-ridden and yet genuinely religious in an orthodox way. Philip Repyngdon, formerly his confessor, who had remonstrated with Henry about the rotten state of the country, was now Bishop of Lincoln and came over to see him accompanied by a large party. Six years later Repyngdon was to appoint Thomas Chaucer, a son of the poet, as Speaker and Seneschel of the castle and town of Banbury for life.[11] Another friend to visit Henry was the Lincolnshire peer William Lord Willoughby, who had accompanied Henry to Prussia and to Ravenspur on his landing in 1399.

We hear of Lady Lucia Visconti again in the summer of 1406. She was Henry's youthful adorer, who had fallen in love with him when Earl of Derby and vowed that, unless she could have him, she would never marry elsewhere. However, she was contracted by marriage to Edmund Holland, Earl of Kent, in Milan, and later married to him on June 24th 1407 in the Church of St. Mary Overy. Henry himself gave away the bride, a grand social event where after the wedding the guests went to the Palace of Henry Beaufort, since 1404 Bishop of Winchester, for a lavish banquet, "a wondir grete fest" according to *The Brut*. Edmund Holland, constantly in debt, was appointed Admiral of the Fleet, but was killed whilst besieging Bréhat in Brittany during September 1408. "This Lucye," relates Bernard Holland.[12] "after the death of her husbande, by whom she had none issue, was moved by the King to marry hys bastard brother the Erle of Dorset (actually he had been made legitimate), a man very aged, and evil-visaged whose person neyther satisfied her phantasie nor whose face pleased her appetite." Nor would Henry IV with his pock-marked face have now appealed to her. However, after she had satisfied her alleged wanton desire by taking for her new husband Henry Mortimer, "a goodly young esquire and a beautiful bachelor", the King was so angry with her for marrying without his licence that he fined Lucia heavily, a fine lately remitted by Henry V, who created her husband a knight and appointed him to important offices in England and Normandy. Lucia survived until the reign of the infant Henry VI, dying during April 1424 and being interred in the Church of the Austen Friars in Bread Street.

There are indications that Archbishop Arundel, the Chancellor from January 1407 until December 1409, had forgiven Henry for disregarding his advice concerning the execution of the Archbishop of York and for his duplicity. At nineteen the Prince of Wales during December 1406 and later, after temporarily leaving Wales where he had enjoyed some success, was a leading member of the Council, working at first harmoniously with Arundel and later in violent opposition to him. In February 1407 the Council, presumably instigated by Archbishop Arundel, confirmed the Act of Parliament passed ten years before when King Henry's half-brothers, the Beauforts, were legitimized. What incensed them, however, were the words added to the original document, "excepta dignitate regale". Unnecessary it might be thought, because Henry's four legitimate sons might all have heirs. Henry Beaufort became even more antagonistic to Arundel and the three Beaufort brothers were later to support the Prince of Wales in opposition to the Archbishop.

Trials by battle were fairly common during the reign of Henry IV. *The Brut* describes such a battle: "Yn the VIII yere of King Harres reign" between a Welsh clerk and a knight named Sir Percival Sowden. The clerk accused Sir Percival of treason, so there ensued a fight to the death. At last the clerk was forced to yield and after being "despoyled of his armeour", taken to be hung at Tyburn. The victim was adjudged innocent of treason. During August 1407 the King was present at Nottingham at another Trial by Battle between John Bolomer, a Bordeaux seamster, and Bertrand Ursana, a merchant of the same city. When the combatants were fully prepared, the Constable of England cried "Laisser les aller, laissez les aller et faire leur devoir." French was then the language of chivalry. Both men fought for a long time so bravely that the King cried "Ho, ho, ho", a signal for them to stop. He declared that neither Bolomer or Ursana should die, for they were loyal. However, the spectators probably felt cheated, for duels of this nature were popular entertainment.

When one considers the hardships of medieval travel, one can but marvel how often in the early fifteenth century pilgrims trudged to Rome or went by ship from Dartmouth or Plymouth to visit the shrine of St. James at Santiago de Compostela in Spain. According to Wylie, the pilgrims were often criminals convicted of rape. For the long, arduous journey to Jerusalem, the Holy City, it was customary to voyage to Jaffa. The travellers would play cards or dice, while many suffered from pangs of sea-sickness, fleas and rats. They would experience terrible fears, never knowing whether they would reach their destination alive. Passengers would lie on top of one another, packed in dark cabins. They made their way to Ramleh, and on foot from Jaffa to Jerusalem which usually took a fortnight. Most pilgrims were pious and behaved discreetly, but four grey friars provoked the authorities at Jerusalem by rashly telling them that the Koran was all lies and the Prophet a glutton and a murderer. Not unnaturally offence was taken, and they were beaten to death, their bodies being cut up and thrown into a fire.

A favoured pilgrim such as Richard Beauchamp, Earl of Warwick, son of the Lord Appellant, who had been banished by Richard II, could indulge in every luxury. On his travels (1407) he went with a chaplain and many attendants, taking English cloth, and "furred gowns of black Puke", to give as presents. Making a leisurely stay in Paris during May, he enjoyed the company of the Scottish Earl of March. After visiting Rome he fought a tournament at Verona and travelling with a French herald to Lombardy, he reached Venice in August 1408. From Venice to Beyrout he voyaged in a Beyrout galley, luxurious enough, for the whole of the armoury, the cook-house and the poop-scandler had been reserved for him and those who accompanied him. From Jaffa[13] he made for Jerusalem, to be received by the Patriarch's Deputy. After making his offering, the Saracen Sultan of Egypt bestowed many honours on him. Warwick, a hard soldier, returned to England to give his friend Henry IV notable service, but he was later of the Prince of Wales's party. Such were the vivid contrasts of medieval travel.

At a Parliament held at Gloucester on October 24th 1407, Archbishop Arundel took a leading part as Chancellor, preaching the sermon and praising the King for maintaining the liberties of the Church and of all his subjects. Arundel might eulogize Henry for showing justice and mercy, but he had been harsh on many occasions, possibly from necessity, as disorder was prevalent in the kingdom through Henry's reign.

Thomas Chaucer, a son of Geoffrey the poet and his wife Philippa, a sister of Katherine Swynford, now became Speaker, serving in this capacity on five occasions between 1407-21. He was very acquisitive, even obtaining enormous estates at the start of his career in the Thames Valley, yet while he sat as a Knight of the Shires, he never became a Knight. In many ways he was an outstanding Speaker, handling the Commons with considerable skill. He excelled, too, in diplomacy, inheriting, perhaps, the gift from his father, but of his literary genius he had nothing. Like all medieval speakers, he asked to be excused from office. When this was refused, he then asked to speak under the protestation that if he said anything displeasing to the King, he might be forgiven. Henry immediately assented. By his marriage he became Lord of the manor of Ewelme in Oxfordshire, acquiring considerable wealth from his office.

Sir John Tiptoft, Thomas Chaucer's predecessor as Speaker, prospered mightily on relinquishing his post, being appointed Keeper of the Wardrobe, Treasurer of the Royal Household and Chief Butler. During 1407, on the forfeiture of Owain Glyn Dŵr's extensive estates in South Wales, he was rewarded with some of those lands. He possessed the King's confidence, attending as a witness when he made a will on January 21st 1408 at Greenwich. Henry also used him in a diplomatic capacity to negotiate with the envoys of the Hanse towns and persuade them to postpone their demands for repayment of a loan advanced to the King. Three years later he was created Steward and Constable of the castles of Brecknock, Cantresell, Grosmont and Skenfrith.

Owain Glyn Dŵr, during the long war he waged against the English, suffered serious disadvantages. Not only did he lack to some extent sea-power, but the seaport merchants were bitterly hostile to him. Caernarvon Castle, famous for its investiture of the

Princes of Wales, successfully resisted sieges by Owain and his French allies in 1403 and 1404. For the English, Chester was an important source of supply for artillery and other necessities of war. In March and June 1403, before the Welsh rebels successfully besieged Harlech, a total of 50 bows and 54 sheaves of arrows were supplied to Harlech Castle from Chester. Another important source of supply for these primitive weapons was Hereford.[14] One factor militating in favour of the English were their superior means of destruction. Great guns were transported all the way by sea to the coast of Cardigan, while cannon was very effectively used when the castles of Harlech and Aberystwyth were later recovered.

The old Earl of Northumberland and Lord Bardolf, now fugitives in Scotland, fearing that they might be handed over by Robert Stuart, Duke of Albany, the Regent, who was constantly negotiating with Henry, escaped to Wales to join Owain where they were given a warm welcome. Owain, engrossed in his own troubles, could give Northumberland little comfort, so he and Bardolf fled to Brittany, taking refuge in Paris and Flanders where they plotted against Henry IV. In Paris, the noblemen, much impoverished, pleaded for assistance from Charles VI, promising that they would henceforward serve the King and become his men, but Adam of Usk relates that the influence of the Duke of Orléans weighed against them.[15]

While staying as fugitives in the lovely city of Bruges, Northumberland lodged in the ancient monastery of St. Bartholomew of Eeckhout (demolished in 1798) and Bardolf in a hospice in the centre of the city. Adam relates that he often held converse with them, causing Henry to be even more indignant against them. He relates in his hypocritical way, "but God visited mine heart, and I bethought me: 'Adam, thus beset in a maze, place thyself in the hand of the Lord.'". He was to bide his time and eventually to return to Wales to join my Lord of Powis, a peer friendly to Henry IV. He landed at the port of Barmouth during 1408, pretending to embrace Owain's cause. There is a typical account of a terrible storm in Bruges, "a ball of fire, greater than a large barrel, lighting up as it were, the whole world." Men feared lest the city should be destroyed.

Another venomous enemy of King Henry, Louis Duke of Orléans, was assassinated in the streets of Paris on November 23rd 1407. John the Fearless, a small ugly man, had succeeded his father as Duke of Burgundy three years earlier and he, too, hated Orléans worse than Philip the Bold. A messenger saluted Orléans with a false summons requiring his immediate presence at the Hostel de St. Pol by Charles VI. It was a dark winter evening as the Duke sallied forth about eight o'clock, with five attendants and two linkmen. Orléans was in a light-hearted mood as he ambled along with his black-furred cloak flung loosely over his shoulders, singing a gay air as he flapped his glove. Suddenly seven or eight visored men sprang out at him from an empty house and with a violent blow cleft his skull, stabbing their daggers into his face and body. There is no doubt that John the Fearless was the real instigator of the murder, though he attended the funeral and paid the dead nobleman every mark of respect. Orléans' character was a strange mixture of religious devotion and debauchery. In the early fifteenth century no great lord displayed more love for pleasure and luxury and he was fond of necromancy. Yet he had his cell in the common dormitory of the Celestins, where he endured the privations of monastic life.[16]

The Orléanist party or the Armagnacs was deprived of its head. Armagnac is a county in Gascony and the Counts of that name were a very ancient family. After Louis's assassination, his heir Charles married the Count of Armagnac's daughter as his second wife. France became more and more riven between the rival factions and it was the policy of Henry IV and his government to play off one faction against another.

The winter of 1407-08, called "The great Frost and Ice", was the worst for one hundred years. From December to March, England and much of Europe was covered with snow. The Earl of Northumberland and Lord Bardolf could not have chosen a worse time for their rebellion. By the end of December they had returned to Scotland and were soon able to muster a small force consisting of loyal Percy retainers, disaffected persons and various church-men such as the Prior of Hexham, Lewis Bifort, Bishop of Bangor, the Abbot of Halesowen, several of the monks of Fountains Abbey and chaplains from Topcliffe, one of the Percy strongholds in Yorkshire.

It seems likely that Northumberland harboured hopes that the Sheriff of Yorkshire, Sir Thomas Rokeby, with whom he had once served and with whom he had corresponded, might side with him. Rokeby, however, commanded a small army at Knaresborough and confronted the rebel lords at Bramham Moor near Tadcastle in Yorkshire, intending to profit from their defeat. Fighting with desperate courage like a lion, old Northumberland fell in the battle on February 19th 1408, while Bardolf was fatally wounded and later died from his wounds, having been captured with his servants, John Lesingham and John Smethies, both from Suffolk. The body of the Earl of Northumberland was beheaded and quartered in the customary barbarous way, while Lord Bardolf's body was quartered and his head set over one of the gates of Lincoln. With the defeat at Bramham Moor, the fortunes of the Percys touched a new low point. Rokeby was rewarded with Northumberland's manor of Spofforth. On April 8th, King Henry after travelling rapidly from Leicester, Nottingham and Bishopthorpe, reached Pontefract. The churchmen involved in the rebellion met various fates. The Abbot of Halesowen was hanged, while the Prior of Hexham was tried for treason, but pardoned, and Bishop Bifort of Bangor after imprisonment at Windsor was freed.

So, after eight years of rebellion and intermittent strife, Henry experienced an uneasy peace in his kingdom, but it had been at great cost to his health.

When Westmoreland, married to Henry's half-sister, bore him the welcome intelligence that Archbishop Scrope's and Mowbray's rebellion had been crushed in Shakespeare's *Henry IV*, Part II, to be followed by Harcourt with the news of Northumberland's defeat at Bramham Moor, Henry can find little joy, for his health has been fatally undermined:

> Will Fortune never come with both hands full
> But write her fair words still in foulest letters?...
> I should rejoice now at this happy news,
> And now my sight fails, and my brain is giddy...[17]

IX   Defeat of Owain Glyn Dŵr

The recovery of the important castles of Aberystwyth and Harlech was vigorously pursued during the late summer, autumn and winter (1407-08).[1] Acting as King Henry's deputy in North and South Wales, the Prince of Wales had a formidable force under his command. His captains included the Duke of York (Edward of Rutland), the Earl of Warwick, recently returned from a pilgrimage to Jerusalem, Thomas Lord Carew and Sir John Carew, and Lord Berkeley, the admiral who transported Queen Joanna from Brittany, directed operations against Aberystwyth Castle. Insufficient credit has been given Gilbert Lord Talbot, for he was largely responsible for the recovery of Harlech Castle.[2] He was later to play an important part in the pacification of Wales, being appointed to treat with Glyn Dŵr and his son Maredudd when they finally submitted. He received rich rewards, the justiceanships of Chester and North Wales for his services.

The Welsh garrison at Aberystwyth under the command of Rhys ap Griffith ap Llewellyn ap Jenkin made a stubborn resistance for some time against powerful odds. However, Henry IV's own 4½ ton gun was transported from Nottingham via Hereford, together with 538 lbs. of powder, 971 lbs. of saltpetre and 303 lbs. of sulphur, with a powerful gun called 'the messenger'. At Harlech a cannon was known as 'the King's daughter'. Owain was highly indignant when he heard that Rhys had signed a treaty with Prince Henry and threatened to behead him.[3] He hastened to the castle and for some time stoutly resisted the English assault. For the present Prince Henry abandoned the fight, only to resume the siege in the summer (1408) when he succeeded in capturing the castle. Meanwhile Harlech Castle remained uncaptured.

Among those serving Prince Henry in Wales was the celebrated Sir John Oldcastle, the most prominent Lollard of his age, who had represented Herefordshire in the Parliament of 1404, becoming Sheriff in 1407. This county since the last decade of the fourteenth century had been a hotbed of Lollardy[4], though it is not known when Oldcastle became a Lollard. As a trusted servant of Henry IV in the Welsh marches, he had assisted the Constable of Kidwelly Castle on the Carmarthenshire coast, with 40 lances and 120 archers during the September following the Battle of Shrewsbury. Henry had so much confidence in him that he gave him *carte blanche* to pardon or to punish such of his Welsh tenants as were rebels. Through his wife he inherited the title of Lord Cobham in 1409.

Possibly Oldcastle was a boon companion of the Prince of Wales in his escapades in his youth. John Bale, who wrote an early biography[5], records that "His youthe was full of wanton wildenesse before he knew ye scriptures". Oldcastle himself confessed, "that in my frayle youthe I offended the lords and most greevously in pryde, wrathe and glottonye, in covetousnesse and in lechere". The anti-Wycliffites, however, condemned him as a "myghtye mayntener of other heretyques...chylde of iniquyte and darknesse." It was left to writers in the sixteenth century to give a more favourable portrait. John Foxe in *Actes and Monuments*, echoing Bale[6] describes him as a "principall favourer, receiver and maintainer of Lollards, a Protestant hero, scholar, philosopher, man of virtue and religious convert." How far he served as a model for Shakespeare's great comic creation Falstaff is controversial and does not concern us here. The scenes in Eastcheap in *King Henry the Fourth*, Part II, are a wonderful evocation of life in that period. Those familiar with the play will remember the scene when the Hostess reproaches Falstaff for making a promise to marry her "when the Prince broke thy head for liking his father to a singing-man of Windsor."

The decline of Oldcastle's fortunes began in 1410, largely owing to his unlicensed preaching of Lollardy. It was even suspected that he tried to convert the Prince of Wales and he was already in grave trouble two weeks before Henry IV's death when evidence was mounting that he was a heretic.[7] The persecution of Lollards was to become even more savage in the reign of Henry V, and Sir John was to be burnt to death in the presence of the Lord John of Lancaster, now Duke of Bedford.

138

Henry V's early portrait in the National Portrait Gallery, if it is a real likeness, resembles a priest rather than a warrior. According to E.F. Jacob, a Frenchman Jean Fusoris, visiting Winchester in his reign wrote in 1415 that Thomas, Duke of Clarence, his younger brother, really looked a soldier, while Henry had the noble stature and the distinguished manners of a lord but seemed more suited to the church than to war. Henry's hard life aged him prematurely and he later grew a beard. Curiously enough he did not resemble a traditional Englishman. Instead, there seemed some trait in him of an Este or a Gonzaga, so that his diplomacy may be described as tortuous and Italianate. He undoubtedly inherited an interest in moral and theological questions from his father.

His reputation for wildness and debauchery in his youth is so frequently mentioned in early chronicles that it must have some substance. It was natural enough for him after months of harsh warfare in Wales to sow his wild oats in London. He had a town house, once the Black Prince's, Coldharbour near London Bridge, next to the Church of All Hallows the Less. Possibly some of his escapades have been confused with the adventures of his younger brothers Thomas and Humphrey, for it is known that they were involved in a midnight brawl at a tavern in Eastcheap on June 23rd 1410[8] and hot-headed Thomas was so quarrelsome that the authorities found it difficult to restrain him.

Most of the early chronicles such as *Vita Henrici Quinti* by Tito Livio, dwell on Henry's debaucheries as Prince of Wales, while *The Brut* states that "he fylle and yntendyd gretly to ryot...and dyvas Ientylmen and Ientylwommen followyd his wyll." Enguerrard de Monstrelet's *Chronicles*[9] provide authentic information that Prince Henry tried on his father's crown on one celebrated occasion when Henry IV lay desperately ill. The fourth Earl of Ormonde, whom Henry V knighted at Agincourt, tells how the Prince would lie in ambush to rob his own receivers. Later he was to become even more bigoted than his father and hostile to the Lollards.

Henry IV's relations with his eldest son undoubtedly deteriorated from 1407 onwards. Throughout history the relations between Kings and the Princes of Wales have always been sensitive and complex. One thinks of Edward I enraged with his son

Edward, our first Prince of Wales, for his conduct with Piers Gaveston. King Henry was jealous of his eldest son's success in Wales and resented the great resort of people to him. He later suspected, perhaps wrongly, that Prince Henry had designs on his throne and, influenced by the Beauforts, intended to depose him. Despite his sudden seizures Henry IV would never have agreed to such a drastic course, for he was determined to cling to power.

On occasion, great mental strain would prostrate him physically. Of those around him he could trust Archbishop Arundel, Westmoreland, Warwick and faithful household servants such as John Norbury and Sir Thomas Erpingham of a Norfolk family. They remained his best friends.

When incapacitated during the last few years of his life, he left the government in the capable hands of Archbishop Arundel. Henry was so ill, while staying at Mortlake, that many people thought he was dead. Continued grief and remorse for the execution of Archbishop Scrope and for his earlier crime of seizing Richard II's throne, tortured his mind. His illness could well have been psychological.

Arundel was preoccupied by three burning questions: the great schism in the church, the urgent need to heal it and his obsession at home to suppress the Lollards. It was planned to send the delegates of a general council to Pisa, including Robert Hallam, Bishop of Salisbury, and Henry Chichele, Bishop of St. Davids (a future Archbishop of Canterbury). The Council opened its session in Pisa on March 25th 1409, when both rival Popes were deposed and Alexander V was elected to be succeeded by Baldassare Cossa as John XXIII.

The French contemporary historian Enguerrard de Monstrelet has one excellent quality - he is absolutely impartial when he refers to the leaders of the two factions, Burgundians and Armagnacs. He praises or blames them according to the merits of their actions. His style is, however, rather heavy, lacking Jean Froissart's charm and glimpse of character. He occasionally shows sentiment. In 1411, Charles VI, in league with John the Fearless, Duke of Burgundy, ordered by an express edict, that all of the Orléans party should be attacked as enemies throughout the kingdom. It was a pitiful thing, wrote Monstrelet, to hear the miserable complaints of the persecution and sufferings of individuals. Three thousand combatants marched to Bicêtre, a very handsome house belonging to the Duke of Berri (who was of the Orléans party) and from hatred of the said Duke, they destroyed and villainously demolished the whole house except the walls.

For some time King Henry was wise enough to pursue an impartial policy between Burgundians and Armagnacs.[10] He actually caused it to be proclaimed by sound of trumpets in Calais that none of his subjects of whatever rank should in any way interfere between the two factions, nor serve either of them by arms or otherwise, under pain of death or confiscation of fortune. Later he changed his policy, agreeing to send to the Dukes of Berri, Orléans and their party, eight thousand men under the command of his second son, the Lord Thomas, recently created Duke of Clarence. The Prince of Wales always favoured the Burgundians.

The surrender of the castles of Aberystwyth and Harlech was an overwhelming blow for Owain Glyn Dŵr. Harlech held out until January 1409. For a long time the Welsh deprived of water and without faggots for heating, refused to surrender. Sir Edmund Mortimer, Owain's son-in-law, died of starvation during the siege of Harlech, while Owain's wife Margaret, Katherine Mortimer, and Lionel (Sir Edmund's son and two of his daughters) were forced to surrender and were sent to the Tower of London. What a pitiable end for Sir Edmund Mortimer, for whom a brilliant future had been predicted!

Katherine Mortimer languished in prison until 1413, when she died, to be buried in St. Swithin's Churchyard. The fate of Margaret, Owain's widow, is unknown, but she existed in dire poverty.

Owain, indomitable in defeat, survived as a guerrilla leader and fugitive in the mountains, lying miserably in caves and in thickets according to Adam of Usk. He made one last desperate raid on the Shropshire border in 1410. In vain, for he was defeated and three of his most loyal captains were captured. Philip Scudamore was hung at Shrewsbury, while Rhys ap Griffith of Cardigan was executed in London and Rhys ap Tudor of Anglesea suffered the same fate at Chester. Even as late as 1411 Owain remained troublesome, for Henry IV was obliged to maintain expensive troops in Wales. After the King's death on March 20th 1413, his son, now Henry V, offered the Welsh rebels, still under arms, a pardon, provided they submitted. The great rebel proudly refused.

Of Owain Glyn Dŵr's last years and mysterious death we know little. One of his daughters married Sir John Croft, an ancestor of Lord Croft of Croft Castle. Owain, however, sought refuge with his daughter Alice, married to a local squire John Scudamore, who lived at Kentchurch in the Golden Valley on the Welsh borders. He found shelter with a friend, and one can see to this day the celebrated Owain's Tower where he stayed. Outside the sombre bedroom, smacking of the medieval age, there is a dark turreted staircase. Alone with his thoughts, the intrepid rebel would not have cared to be reminded that in Grosmont, a few miles away, he had experienced one of his greatest reverses. Monnington, nestling in apple orchards, also claims the privilege of having harboured the fugitive. Where did he die? Nobody knows. A visitor to Snowdonia gazing from afar at the purple mountains, might imagine Owain alive today, watching over his people, ever vigilant to keep the flame of rebellion alive. The end of the conflict saw savage legislation being passed by the English Parliament against the Welsh.

Another Welshman, Adam of Usk, in exile earlier, relates after a long period of disgrace how he succeeded in being pardoned by Henry IV, but not till 1411. The duplicity he employed to achieve his ends hardly reflects credit on him. He had been for a while in contact with Richard de Bruges, created Lancaster King of Arms, in whom he confided. Pretending that he was a supporter of Glyn Dŵr, a cunning ruse, Adam succeeded in escaping to the port of St. Pol in Brittany. Then in secrecy facing numerous hazards, Adam travelled by boat to Barmouth (its native name is Abermaw) in Wales. Hiding in the surrounding hills and caves and having to endure many hardships, including sleepless nights with scarcely anything to eat or drink, Adam sent a message to my Lord of Powis, his patron, a friend of the King, asking for safe conduct. This nobleman was absent from Wales at this time, having taken for a second wife Elizabeth, daughter of Sir John Berkeley of Beverstone, Gloucester. When Owain discovered that Adam of

Usk was acting as a double agent, he tried his damnedest to apprehend him, but after many misadventures and the mortification of being shunned by former friends, he was pardoned. My Lord Powis and David Holbach, member of Parliament for Shrewsbury and a founder of Oswestry Grammar School, acted as his intermediaries with Henry IV. So the exiled chronicler returned to England, rejoicing and praising God. He joined the household of Archbishop Arundel at Canterbury. He died some years later, to be interred in the Priory Church of St. Mary in Usk, his birthplace, a Benedictine priory founded by Richard Strongbow about 1160. There is a plaque to his memory.

At the beginning of January 1409, John Badby of Evesham, a tailor by profession, was examined before the Bishop of Worcester for his heretical opinions and given a year to recant, but he refused to do so. He was now brought to trial before the convocation of Canterbury sitting at Blackfriars. Confronting him were Archbishop Arundel, Bishop Henry Beaufort, Bishop Chichele and others. Also present were the Duke of York, Thomas Beaufort, the Chancellor and Lord de Roos. He maintained that the priest's words could not change bread into the body of Christ, that he would never believe that a priest had more power to do so than any rack-raker in Bristol.[1] He was imprisoned, giving him more time for reflection to recant. Pointing to the Duke of York he declared that he or any living person was worth more than the sacramental bread, however consecrated by any priest. As he spoke, a spider crawled on his face, causing him to make a fresh outburst. He exclaimed that the bread was worth less than even a spider or a toad, for they at least were alive, while the bread was dead matter. Archbishop Arundel pronounced that Badby was a heretic and that he should be surrendered to the Secular authorities, earnestly praying the Chancellor and the members of the Council that the heretic should be spared the sting of death. He was neither a hardhearted nor a cruel man.[2]

The Council, after delivering Badby to the Sheriff at Smithfield, had him plunged into a flaming barrel. The Prince of Wales, who was becoming increasingly bigoted, was present for he played an active part in suppressing heresy.[3] When the wretched Badby began to scream, Henry had him dragged from the flames and urged him to recant, though he was half dead. Despite being offered a pension, Badby refused, so he was put back in the barrel. Perhaps Badby may have lacked an influential patron to save his life.

Hoccleve, the contemporary poet, sometimes obsequious, praises the Prince too much for his "great tenderness", for he "thirsted sore for his (Badby's) salvation." To the medieval mind the tailor would suffer eternal hell-fire for denying transubstantiation. To us living in the last decade of the twentieth century, we can only be grateful to the brave men who cherished their beliefs so obstinately and strongly that they were prepared to face the most vile torture and suffering. Men are free to believe what they like. Despite the petitioning of many knights in Parliament that the harsh statute of 1401, *De Heretico Comburendo*, should be modified or repealed, the Commons remained submissive and refused to do so.

One of the few people to admire Henry IV for his execution of Archbishop Scrope was John Hus, the great religious reformer, who translated into Czech the heretical teachings of John Wycliffe. Much opposed to clerical laxity, he was excommunicated by the Archbishop of Prague and later tried for heresy. Refusing to recant his opinions, he was burnt at the stake on July 6th 1415.[4] The Lollards suffered similar persecution under Henry V. In London in the same year (two years after the death of his father), a London furrier, John Claydon, was burnt at the stake.

Henry IV's problems in 1409 and for the last four years of his life, were political rather than financial. Freed from his duties in the Welsh marches, there is no doubt that Prince Henry was hungry for power and constantly seeking an opportunity to exercise his talents. Knowing full well that his father was ailing and incapable of firm government, the Prince was convinced that he would make a better king. Certainly Henry IV mistrusted his eldest son during his final years, and there was probably a personal dislike between them. Prince Henry never forgot his early affection for Richard II, as he clearly showed soon after his accession, when he had the deposed King reverently reinterred in Westminster Abbey. He refers to it in some pregnant lines in Shakespeare's *Henry V*:

> Not to-day, O Lord,
> O, not to-day, think not upon the fault
> My father made in compassing the crown!
> I Richard's body have interr'd anew,
> And on it have bestow'd more contrite tears
> Than from it issu'd forced drops of blood.[5]

In its outer form this rivalry between father and son is evident in Henry IV backing the Armagnacs in their bitter feud against the Burgundians and the Prince continuing to support the latter. Another factor may have been Prince Henry's memory of Hotspur before the Battle of Shrewsbury, for many of Harry Percy's servants and followers later joined his service.

During December 1409, there occurred a crisis in the Council between the rival parties. Just before Christmas, the Chancellor, Archbishop Arundel, resigned and before him Tiptoft, the Treasurer.[6] In the new Parliament, Sir Thomas Beaufort served as Chancellor, while Thomas Chaucer again served as Speaker. The Prince of Wales dominated the Council and it consisted of the Bishops of Winchester (Henry Beaufort), Durham and Bath and Wells, the Earls of Arundel and Westmoreland and Lord Burnell, together with Sir Thomas Beaufort. Later the Bishop of St. Davids in Pembrokeshire and the Earl of Warwick became members of the Council, because it was thought that the Earl of Westmoreland and the Bishop of Durham might have to be absent on the northern border.

During this Parliament, dissension arose between the rival factions and a personal quarrel between the Prince and Archbishop Arundel. John Beaufort, Earl of Somerset, died in April 1410 and Prince Thomas, Henry IV's younger son, obtained a dispensation to marry his widow Margaret Holland, daughter of the Earl of Kent. Henry Beaufort, Bishop of Winchester, who was acting as his brother's executor, resented the marriage and relations worsened between the King and the Prince of Wales in their quarrel with the Beauforts. This Parliament was distinctly anti-clerical, for they petitioned for the confiscation of bishops and abbots.

On November 9th 1411 the last Parliament of Henry IV's reign assembled at Westminster. The King's health was so poor that he was unable to travel from Windsor, where he had been for some time, to open Parliament. Sir Thomas Beaufort, the Chancellor, was empowered with this function. About now Henry IV displayed his former energy by frustrating an intrigue by Henry Beaufort to compel him to abdicate and to leave the crown to the Prince of Wales. When accused ten years later, Beaufort never denied fostering such an intrigue, although there is no mention of it in the official records. Others were involved in this affair, including Sir Roger Leche, Steward of the Prince's household, and six knights. They were all sent to the Tower, but soon released.

A case occurred during this Parliament typical of this lawless age. Lord de Roos petitioned the King against William Tirwhyt, a Justice of the King's Bench, who had organized armed men to lie in wait for Lord de Roos with whom he had a serious dispute[7] concerning rights of common at Wramby in Lincolnshire. Archbishop Arundel and Richard Lord Grey were appointed arbiters.

On January 5th 1412, Archbishop Arundel at loggerheads with the Prince of Wales, became Chancellor for the last time, maintaining this office until the death of the King. Despite his ill health, Henry had succeeded in thwarting the Prince of Wales and the Beaufort party. The Prince and his supporters, the Beaufort brothers, Bishop Henry Chichele, Lord Burnell and the Earls of Warwick and Arundel, were all dropped from the Council, while Ralph Neville, Earl of Westmoreland, William Lord de Roos, Henry Bowet, Archbishop of York, all the King's friends, became members of the new Council. It represented a victory for Henry IV.

The account of the serious discord between Henry IV and the Prince of Wales owes much to the translator of a work by an Italian scholar, Titus Livio.[8] Titus depended a lot on the firsthand accounts of James Butler, Earl of Ormonde, a friend of the future Henry V, a nobleman deeply interested in history. Titus was a native of Forli, about 40 miles from Ferrara in Italy, whose patron was Henry IV's youngest son Humphrey, later created Duke of Gloucester. Indeed it was at Humphrey's suggestion that Titus Livio wrote his early *Life of Henry V*. In his own account the chronicler John Stow makes full use of the translator of Livio's writings; so does the chronicler Otterbourne in these words: "Meanwhile Prince Henry, offended by the King's friends, who, it is said, sowed discord between father and son, wrote to all parts of the realm, endeavouring to refute all the machinations of his detractors. And to make his good faith more manifest about the feast of SS Peter and Paul (June 29th 1412) he came to the King his father with a great company of his friends and followers, the like of which had never been seen before. After a short space he was graciously received by the King, of whom he asked this alone that if his slanderers were convicted of falsehood they should be punished not in accordance with their deserts, but with such measure as was fitting. The King seemed to assent to his request, but said that they ought to await a Parliament, when those persons might be punished by the judgements of their peers."

Most other accounts attribute the ill relations between father and son to the events of the Parliament of November 1411. Stow refers to the constant mischief-making by Pickthanks sewing division about the Court.

The actual scene between King Henry and his son seems to have occurred between June 30th and July 8th 1412, when they were both in London. In early July it is known that Henry IV was at the Priory of St. John at Clerkenwell and from July 3rd to July 8th at the Bishop's Palace at St. Pauls, whence he removed to Rotherhithe on the Thames. According to the Earl of Ormonde, an eyewitness, the meeting was in Westminster and it is possible that the King came there from the Bishop's Palace. John Stow's account, derived from Ormonde, is very colourful. He relates: "Prince Henry was apparelled in a gowne of blew satten, full of small oilet holes, at everie hole the needle hanging by a silke thred with which it was sewed. About his arme he wore a hounds collar set full of SS of gold, and the tirets likewise being of the same metall." A strange disguise for a Prince of Wales.

The King, "greenouslie diseased" as described by Stow, had been carried in his chair to his privy chamber. The Prince on his knees, humbly enough, told his father that he knew very well that he would punish any man within this realm, "of whome you should stand in fear..." Taking his dagger, the Prince told his father to ease his mind of all suspicion of him and plunge the dagger into his heart, for "his life was not so deare to him, that he wished to live one daie with his displeasure." There then occurred an emotional scene culminating in a reconciliation when the King embraced the Prince of Wales, casting away the dagger and after shedding many tears, admitting that he had held him partly in suspicion, but that it was unjustified. Henceforward he would in no wise hold him in mistrust, influenced by his detractors.

Earlier his enemies had accused the Prince of misappropriating the money assigned for Calais, since 1347 England's military and commercial bridgehead in Northern France, where many English had settled. In 1410 Prince Henry had appointed himself Captain of Calais, and after examining the finances of that town, discovered the low morale of the garrison, amounting to mutiny, for their pay of £9,000 was in arrears.[9] The Prince indignantly refuted the accusations and the Council then declared that the charges of misusing the funds were false.

During his last years Henry IV preferred to stay at riverside palaces such as Rotherhithe for the summer, where he could travel by barge, an easy form of travel for a sick man. At Rotherhithe he created his younger son Thomas, now in high favour, Duke of Clarence, an unlucky title, during July 1412, and as if to balance this honour, he created Sir Thomas Beaufort, Earl of Dorset, a member of the Prince of Wales's party. Earlier in May, the King had agreed to send a large expedition consisting of 1,000 men-at-arms and 3,000 archers to aid the Armagnacs (Orléanists) against the Burgundians. A typical Plantagenet, brave, though rash in temperament and always desirous to emulate his elder brother, Clarence and his men marched to Blois, where they heard that their help was no longer required because the Armagnacs had given in to the Burgundians. The expedition was very expensive, costing about £600 per day, or £6,000 per month. Declaring that they wished to be compensated for their trouble in embarking on this enterprise, Clarence's men plundered, killed and looted as they went. According to Jean Juvénal[10] the French historian, Clarence became richer by 40,000 crowns and a jewelled cross worth 15,000 crowns, while the Duke of York, who was serving in this campaign, acquired 5,000 crowns and a cross valued at 40,000 crowns. From the first, the Prince of Wales had disliked the purpose of this expedition, for he sided with the Burgundians.

Throughout Henry IV's reign we hear of vile weather conditions. During 1412, according to one chronicle, "Upon the twelfth day of October, were three flouds in the Thames, the one following up on the other and no ebbing betweene: which thing no man then living could remember the like to be seen."

Ever since, as Earl of Derby, Henry had made a pilgrimage to Jerusalem over twenty years earlier, the longing to return there obsessed his mind. He prayed that he would have sufficient strength to make the journey possible, but he was ill before

Christmas 1412. A Council was held in the White Friars in London when an order was made for the provision of ships and galleys to undertake a voyage to the Holy Land for the recovery of the City of Jerusalem from the hands of the Infidels. On October 21st, Henry was still taking an active interest in government, confirming that 100 marks should be spent on repairs to the walls of Berwick, and discussing with his Council the problem of Ireland, and the pressing need of paying the arrears due to the Prince of Wales's troops in Wales.[11] In the same way that Richard Whittingdon, former Mayor of London, had once helped Richard II with a loan, so did he now make an offer of £1,000 to pay some of the troops in Wales. But the finances of Calais were the most important matter to be considered by the Council.

Henry's last Christmas was passed at Eltham, and about this time he seemed to recover his strength; but the skin disease from which he suffered was as virulent as ever. The King during the last months of his life was a very worried man, fearful that the strained relations between the Prince of Wales and Thomas of Clarence might provoke his younger son to attempt to usurp the throne. Stow relates[12] that the King summoned the Prince of Wales to his presence, and told him: "My sonn, I feare me sore after my departure from this life, some discorde shall sourd (grow) and arise betwixt thee and Thomas, thy Brother, the Duke of Clarence, whereby the realme may be brought to distraction and misserie, for I knowe you both to be of so greate stomache and courage, wherefore I feare that he throughe his high mynde will make some enterprise against thee intendinge to usurpe uppon thee, wch I knowe thie stomake may not abide easily." The King for a long time had bitterly reproached himself "for ever charging himself with the crowne of this realm." The Prince now assured his father that he hoped with God's will and pleasure he would continue to reign over us for a long time. It must have seemed obvious to the Prince that his father might die at any moment. He told Henry IV that if God provided that he should succeed him, he would honour and love his three brothers so long as they were true, faithful and obedient to him as to their sovereign lord. If they were to conspire or rebel against him, he would execute judgement upon them as he would upon the worst or most humble person in the kingdom.

The King was vastly relieved by the Prince's assurance, saying according to Stow, "My deare and well belouved son, with this answere thou hast delivered me of a great and ponderous agony." Indeed Henry IV need not have tormented himself, for Clarence gave Henry V loyal service when he succeeded him, fighting for his brother at Harfleur in 1415 and elsewhere. However, attempting to emulate Henry in his victory at Agincourt, Thomas of Clarence rashly attacked the French with cavalry only, an act which would have incurred the censure of Henry if not worse, had not Clarence been killed in this battle at Baugé (1421).

The King's homily to his eldest son would seem genuine enough. He admonished him to administer justice impartially, "and in no wise suffer people not to be oppressed long, that call upon thee for justice, but redresse oppressions and indifferently and without delay, for no persuasions or flatteries, or of them that be partiall, or such as use to have theire hands replenished wth giftes"; he also advised his heir to keep his kingdom in tranquillity, something he had never himself been able to achieve. And King Henry touched on many other matters.

Henry IV's death in the Jerusalem Chamber of Westminster Abbey has been described by many chroniclers, most vividly by Shakespeare. The Jerusalem Chamber was at this period part of the Abbot's lodging. According to Fabian, he was taken with his last sickness whilst saying his prayers before St. Edward's Shrine.

The story that Prince Henry entered his father's chamber in the Palace while he lay grievously ill is based on the French chronicler Monstrelet and is authentic. It was the custom for medieval monarchs to lay their crowns on a pillow beside them as they slept. Thinking that his father was dead, and many of the King's attendants were of the same opinion, for they covered his face with a linen cloth, the Prince of Wales took away the crown. Suddenly awaking from his uneasy sleep, the King noticed that his crown had been removed, so he questioned his attendants, who had to admit that it was the Prince. When summoned to his father's bedside and asked for an explanation, the Prince boldly enough declared: "Sir, to mine and all mens judgements you seemed dead in this world, so I as your next heir apparent took that (the crown) as mine owne, and not as yours." The King sighed deeply as he said in a feeble voice: "Well, faire son, what right I had to it, God knoweth." "Well (said the Prince) if you die King, I will have the garland, and trust to keepe it with the sword against all mine enemies, as you have doone."

Even at the end of his life King Henry's conscience nagged at him, giving him no peace. John Tille, his last confessor, constantly urged him to repent for the execution of Archbishop Scrope and for his usurpation of Richard's throne. According to John Capgrave, the contemporary chronicler, Henry then said that for the former offence he had already obtained absolution from the Pope, but for the taking of the kingdom his sons would never allow him to make that restitution or restoration.

After he had swooned before the shrine in Westminster Abbey, the King was borne by his attendants to the Jerusalem Chamber, so tranquil and beautiful as it is even today, with its tapestries of religious scenes. Temporarily regaining consciousness, he lay in his pallet before a fire while he looked about, bewildered at the strange surroundings. When told it was the Jerusalem Chamber the King murmured: "Praise be to God, for it was foretold me long ago that I would die in Jerusalem." The date was March 20th 1413 and he was aged only forty-six and a few months, already an old man because of his shattered health. His father had died at almost sixty in 1399.

Henry had never cared for the great Abbey Church, like his predecessor, nor had he any reason to be attached to it, for Abbot Colchester and many of the monks had favoured Richard II. Instead, he had evinced a wish to be buried in Canterbury Cathedral. After lying in State at Westminster, his body was conveyed by water to Faversham, and thence to Canterbury. Adam of Usk avows that he had been poisoned, and it is possible "for he had been tormented for five years by rotting of the flesh, by a drying up of the eyes, and by a rupture of the intestines."[13] His coffin was placed in Thomas à Becket's Chapel opposite the resplendent tomb of the Black Prince. His widowed Queen Joanna of Brittany arranged that an altar tomb should be built in this place.

It is strange, but the new King Henry V six years later accused his stepmother, though he had always enjoyed amicable relations with her, of compassing his death. The charge was actually brought by Friar Randolf, a Franciscan of Shrewsbury. It is very likely indeed that Queen Joanna was absolutely innocent of the crime of necromancy or any form of sorcery, least of all any intent to kill Henry, though her father Charles the Bad of Navarre was formerly reputed to be a sorcerer. One of Henry V's biographers[14] opines that the King wanted to get hold of her dowry worth over £6,000. There was a hard, very unattractive side to his character. Joanna languished very agreeably in prison at Leeds Castle in Kent, being allowed plenty of servants. On his deathbed Henry ordered that she should be released, being innocent of the accusations brought against her, and she died in 1437, to be buried beside her husband in Canterbury Cathedral.

Adam of Usk relates that Arundel, Primate of all England, did not survive long his friend Henry IV, dying in early 1413-14. He died unexpectedly of some affection of the throat. Adam seems to have had a strange dream or vision of Arundel "clad in short garments as though about to journey afar...and when I strove with utmost toil to follow him, he handed to me a waxen candle, saying: 'Cut this in twain between us two', and so he vanished from my sight." To die at this time was probably fortunate for Arundel, since Henry V would have had very little need of his services.

Few people regretted the death of Henry IV. His great achievement was to quell the many rebellions against his rule and to pass on peaceably the succession to his throne to a king possessing far more personal magnetism than himself. It is fair, however, to add that Henry V's achievements both in the French wars and in peace at home were partly due to the foundations his father had laid. Henry IV had many of the qualities befitting a medieval king, bravery in battle, courage in adversity, leadership, culture and remarkable diligence, yet in many ways he failed. Perhaps he had too much to contend with. The knowledge that he was an usurper was detrimental to his kingship, and owing to his precarious health he was often compelled to play a rather passive part during his last few years. His conscience gnawed at him ceaselessly. But at least this can be said of him: his dealings with his many parliaments revealed his ability for statesmanship and made for constitutional development, ultimately benefiting the country. However, his claim to the throne was fragile and he was constantly beset by contenders. He also proved incapable of curing many of the abuses that he encountered on usurping the throne. It is interesting to note that Walsingham is one of the few chroniclers to praise Henry, maintaining that he had reigned 'gloriously'. However, it is hard to justify this claim, for Henry IV, primarily a man of action, lacked greatness as a king and the magnetism of his father, John of Gaunt.

In Shakespeare's *Tragedy of Richard II*, the Bishop of Carlisle gave his prophetic warning

> And if you crown him, let me prophesy,
> The blood of England shall manure the ground,
> And future ages groan for this foul act.

And so it was to be.

Notes

Chapter I

1. Harleian MSS 6829, fol. 161. A manuscript of the 17th century.
2. Kirby, *Henry IV of England*, p. 14.
3. Lionel of Clarence had died in Italy (1368).
4. Daughter of Sir Payne Roet of Hainault.
5. *The Usurper King*, Marie Louise Bruce (1987), p. 13.
6. Her story has been told by Anya Seton in a strangeley haunting novel.
7. Almost certainly not an illegitimate son of Edward III.
8. *Henry V as Warlord*, Desmond Seward (1986).
9. *The Usurper King*, Marie Louise Bruce.
10. *Ibid.*, p. 47.
11. *Medieval Lincoln*, Sir Francis Hill, republished 1990, see p. 258, note 4.
12. *Cambridge Medieval History*, Vol. VIII, pp. 362-3.
13. See Armitage-Smith, *John of Gaunt*, also Higden IX.
14. *Knighton* II *et sequendo*.
15. *The Hollow Crown*, Harold F. Hutchison (1961).
16. *Ibid.*, *Medieval Lincoln*, Sir Francis Hill, pp. 258-9.
17. *Ibid.*, Desmond Seward, *Henry V as Warlord*, p. 1.
18. *The Chronicle of Adam of Usk* has been edited by Maunde Thompson (1904).
19. Miss M.V. Clarke, *Fourteenth Century Studies*.
20. See *Knighton's Chronicle*, also Marie Louise Bruce, *The Usurper King*, p.78.
21. *Ibid.*, *The Usurper King*, p. 78.
22. The contemporary pamphlet of Favert is propaganda on behalf of the appellants.
23. See *Chronique de la Traison et Mort de Richard II*, edited by Benjamin Williams.
24. Harl. MSS 4579 fol. 23b.

Chapter II

1. Edited from the originals by Lucy Toulmin Smith (Camden Society) 1894.
2. See Introduction, *Henry IV,* p. XXVIII, *Expeditions to Prussia and the Holy Land*.
3. *Ibid.*, *The Usurper King*, p.111.
4. *Ibid.*, *Henry IV*, p. XXX.
5. *Ibid.*, *The Usurper King*.

6. *Ibid.*, *Henry IV of England*, Kirby.
7. *Ibid.*, *The Usurper King.*
8. *Royal Bastards in Late Medieval England* by Chris Given-Wilson and Alice Curteis (reprinted 1988).
9. *Ibid.*, *Henry IV*. p. XIIX.
10. *Royal and Historical Letters of Henry IV*. Letter written in Latin CXLVII. Appendix 1. Hungleston-Randolf.
11. *Ibid.*, pp. 229-30. *Expeditions to Prussia and the Holy Land.*
12. See C.E. Chamberlin, *The Count of Virtue.*
13. *The Lancashire Hollands* by Bernard Holland (1907).
14. *Ibid.*, *Expeditions to Prussia and the Holy Land.*
15. British Library, Harl. MSS 6829, fol. 161.
16. *Ibid.*, fol. 162.

Chapter III

1. Anthony Goodman, *John of Gaunt*. The exercise of princely power in 14th century Europe (1992), p. 361.
2. *Ibid.*, *The Usurper King*, p. 139.
3. PRO E 101/402/20.
4. *The Oxford Illustrated History of Britain* edited by Kenneth Morgan (1992).
5. *Ibid.*, *John of Gaunt*, p. 157.
6. *The Hollow Crown*, Hutchison.
7. *Ibid.*, *The Usurper King.*
8. *The Brut or the Chronicle of England*, ed. F.W.D. Brie. Early English text.
9. Edited by Benjamin Williams.
10. Known as Cold Harborough and also Poultneys in Henry VI's reign.
11. *Ibid.*, *John of Gaunt.*
12. *Ibid.*, *The Usurper King.*
13. *Ibid.*, note 136, *Chronicle of the Betrayal.*
14. See Vol. II, p. 589, edited by Brie.
15. *Ibid.*, *Chronique de la Traison.*
16. *The Tragedy of Richard II*, Act IV, Scene I, Shakespeare.
17. *Ibid.*, Act I, Scene III.
18. *Ibid.*, p. 718. Vol. II Froissart, Jean. Ed. K. de Lettenhove.
19. *Ibid.*, Kirby, *Henry IV of England.*
20. *Ibid.*, *John of Gaunt.*
21. *Ibid.*, Kirby, *Henry IV of England.*, Rot. Parl. Vol. III, p. 372.
22. Among five Froissart illustrations: The Archbishop visits the Earl of Derby in France. Harleian MSS fol. 4380.
23. *Ibid.*, *Henry IV of England*, p. 54.
24. *Ibid.*, *The Usurper King*, p. 202.
25. Adam of Usk says June 28th.
26. See J. Hardyng, *Chronicle, Medieval Lincoln.*
27. *Traison*, p. 179.

28. Samuel Daniel: The First Fowre Bookes of the Civile Wars Between the Two Houses of Lancaster and Yorke (1595). See Arden, Shakespeare, *Henry IV*, Part II, p. XXXIII.
29. *Traison*, p. 187.
30. Page 174. English text.
31. *Ibid., Henry IV of England.* See *Chronicle of Adam of Usk.*
32. *Ibid., The Usurper King.*
33. Page 216.
34. *The English Historical Review*, Vol. 49, 1934, p. 424.
35. *Ibid.,* Ref. Part III, pp. 422-3. Also *The Hollow Crown*, Hutchison, p. 229.

Chapter IV

1. *Ibid., Henry V as Warlord*, Desmond Seward.
2. *The English Historical Review*, January 1964, No. CCCX. Edited by Denys Hay M.A.
3. *Ibid., Henry IV of England.*
4. *Cambridge Medieval History*, Vol. VIII, pp. 362-3.
5. *Ibid.,* Edited from MS Rawl B. 171 by Friedrich W.D. Brie. Bodleian Library.
6. *Ibid., Adam of Usk. Henry V* by Desmond Seward.
7. *Ibid., The Usurper King*, p. 244.
8. *Ibid., Henry the Fourth of England*, p. 127.
9. See p. 148 Vol. II.
10. See Miss Aston's *Thomas Arundel*: A Study of Church Life in the Reign of Richard II (1961) O.U.P.
11. *The Transformation of Medieval England.* See Chapter 20, *England and Europe* 1399-1422, p. 174.
12. *Ibid., Royal and Historical Letters.*
13. *Ibid., Royal and Historical Letters.*
14. The Journal of the Historical Association, Vol. XLIV-XLV. *Henry IV and the Percies.*
15. *Ibid., Henry IV and the Percies.*
16. Pol. Poems, Vol. II, p. 5.
17. Harrison, *Music in Medieval Britain.* Wylie, Henry IV, Vol. II, p. 487.
18. Act III, Scene I.
19. *Ibid., Royal and Historical Letters of Henry IV.*
20. Statute 5, Henry IV.

Chapter V

1. *Owain Glyndwr Prince of Wales*, Ian Skidmore.
2. See Preface XXIII. *Royal and Historical Letters.*
3. *Owen Glendower.* Bradley, p. 238.
4. *Ibid., Royal and Historical Letters.* pp. 69-70.
5. Eight according to Harleian MSS 1989.

6. An unpublished Oxford University M.Litt. thesis. Submitted in 1980 by W.R.M. Grifith, entitled "The Military Career and Affinity of Henry Prince of Wales 1399-1413." National Library of Wales.
7. E.F. Jacob's *Fifteenth Century*, 1399-1485.
8. *Ibid.*, *The Chronicle of Adam of Usk*, p. 103.
9. *Ibid.*, *Henry IV of England*, Kirby.
10. Date of his birth uncertain 1390-1395. He always shows affection for Picardy.
11. *Ibid.*, *The Chronicles of Enguerrard de Monstrelet*. Translated by Thomas Johnes MDCCCXL.
12. Ditto. Vol. I, p. 239.
13. *Ibid.*, *Royal and Historical Letters,* Henry IV, edited by Hingleston-Randolf, p. 74.
14. Ditto, pp. 87-8.
15. Ditto, pp. 89-90.
16. *Ibid.*, *Owain Glyndwr Prince of Wales*, Ian Skidmore.
17. *Ibid.*, *Henry IV of England*, p. 138.
18. *Ibid.*, *Royal and Historical Letters*, pp. 19-20.
19. *Lives of Queens of England*, Vol. 2, p. 73.
20. *Ibid.*, *Henry IV*, Wylie, Vol. I, p. 310.
21. Cottonian MS, Julius E, 4, fol. 202, British Library, is now divided into three volumes (the Beauchamp Pageants).
22. *Ibid.*, *Henry IV of England*, p. 138.
23. *Ibid.*, *Henry IV of England*.
24. *The Royal Bastards of Medieval England*, Chris Given-Wilson and Alice Curteis (reprinted 1985).

Chapter VI

1. *Ibid.*, *The Chronicle of Adam of Usk* A.D. 1377-1421, p. 126.
2. *Ibid.*, Edited from MS. Rawlinson B. 171 Bodleian Library.
3. *Ibid.*, *Brut*, p. 548.
4. *Ibid.*, *Henry IV and the Percies*. M.W. Bean. Journal of the Historical Association.
5. *Ibid.*, *Henry IV of England*, Kirby.
6. *Ibid.*, *Henry V as Warlord*, Seward.
7. *Ibid.*, *Royal and Historical Letters*, 4 Henry IV, pp. 150-1.
8. *Battlefields of England*, Lieutenant-Colonel Burnes.
9. *Ibid.*, *Henry IV,* Part I, Act IV, Scene I.
10. First part of *Henry IV*, Act I, Scene I.
11. There is an interesting relic in the Posterne Tower, found on the battlefield of Shrewsbury and presented to the Second Duke of Northumberland (1787).
12. *Ibid.*, *Plantagenet England*, edited by Elizabeth Hallam, p. 64.
13. Chapter VII, Vol. I, p. 14.
14. *Ibid.*, *Royal and Historical Letters* Henry IV, Vol. I, pp. 158-9.

15. *Ibid., Royal and Historical Letters.* Letter written Wednesday, October 3rd 1403.
16. Vol. I (1778) p. 239.

Chapter VII

1. *Ibid.,* Wylie, Vol. III 1407-1410, p. 259.
2. Edward IV and Richard III, sons of Richard Duke of York and Cicely Neville, youngest daughter of the Earl of Westmoreland by his second marriage.
3. *Henry Beaufort,* L.B. Radford, London (1908).
4. *Ibid., Henry IV of England,* Kirby.
5. *Ibid., Royal and Historical Letters* 1 Henry IV, p. 300.
6. Written in Lisbon on December 30th 1403.
7. *Ibid.,* Wylie, Vol. I, p. 431.
8. From March 31st to November 30th 1404.
9. Founded about 1230 in the time of Llewellyn the Great.
10. Adam of Usk, who was certainly acquainted with John Trevor relates his switch of allegiance.
11. *Ibid., Royal and Historical Letters* 5 Henry IV, p. 281.
12. *Ibid., Henry IV of England.,* Kirby.
13. *Ibid.,* Vol I. pp. 208-9, 238-9, 242-4 and 251-408.
14. *Ibid., Henry IV of England,* Kirby.
15. Act III, Scene I, *King Henry the Fourth,* Part I.
16. *Ibid., King Henry the Fourth,* Part I, Act III, Scene I.
17. *Ibid.,* Stubbs Constitutional History of England, Vol. III, p. 50.
18. John Stow, *The Chronicles of England,* 1592.
19. For a fair analysis of the enormity of Henry's behaviour see Bishop Stubbs' history.
20. *Ibid.,* Wylie, Vol. II, p. 345.
21. *Ibid., Thomas Arundel,* Miss Aston.
22. See Hardyng's Verse account.
23. *Ibid.,* Wylie, Vol. II, p. 345.
24. See Hardyng's Verse.

Chapter VIII

1. *Ibid.,* Wylie, Vol. II, p. 19.
2. An unpublished Oxford University M.Litt. thesis submitted in 1980 by W.R.M. Griffiths entitled "The Military Career and Affinity of Henry Prince of Wales 1399-1413".
3. *Ibid.,* National Library of Wales, Aberystwyth, North Wales. 1399-1413.
4. *Henry IV of England,* Kirby.
5. *The English Parliament in the Middle Ages* C. 1377-1422, Davies Denton.
6. *Ibid., The Plantagenet Encyclopaedia.*
7. Edited by Mary Everett Green (1846).

8. *Ibid.*, another letter in the *Royal and Illustrious Ladies* Collection.
9. *Ibid.*, *Letters of Royal and Illustrious Ladies.* Vol. I, pp. 78-81.
10. *Ibid.*, *Medieval Lincoln*, Sir Francis Hill, Note p. 253.
11. *Ibid.*, *Henry IV of England.*
12. *Ibid.*, *The Lancashire Hollands*, p. 160.
13. Much of this material is indebted to Wylie, *History of Henry IV.*
14. *Owen Glendower*, Arthur Granville Bradley.
15. *Ibid.*, Huizinga, *The Waning of the Middle Ages*, p. 175.
16. *Ibid.*, Shakespeare. Act IV, Scene IV.
17. *Ibid.*, *Henry IV*, Part II.

Chapter IX

1. *Ibid.*, Vol. III, Wylie, p. 112.
2. *Ibid.*, "The Military Career and Affinity of Henry, Prince of Wales 1399-1415."
3. *Ibid.*, *Owain Glyndwr Prince of Wales*, Skidmore.
4. D.N.B. edited Stephen.
5. Briefe Chronycle Concernyng the blessed martyr of Christ Syr John Oldcastle, the Lord Cobham, 1544.
6. *Ibid.*, The Arden Shakespeare *King Henry IV* Part II.
7. Wycliffite tracts were found in the shop of an illuminator in Paternoster Row who confessed that Oldcastle was the owner.
8. *Ibid.*, *Henry V as Warlord*, Seward.
9. Chronicle of Enguerrard de Monstrelet edited Thomas Johnes, p. 211.
10. Ditto.

Chapter X

1. Hoccleve. De Reg 11.7
2. *Ibid.*, Wylie, Vol. III 1407-1410. *Henry the Fourth*, pp. 437-438, 441.
3. Foxe's *Book of Martyrs.*
4. *Ibid.*, *The Plantagenet Encyclopaedia*, p. 101.
5. Act IV, Scene I.
6. *A History of Parliament.* The Middle Ages. Henry IV. Parliament and a Hobbled King, Ronald Butt (1989).
7. *Ibid.*, *A History of Parliament*, p. 482.
8. *The First English Life of King Henry the Fifth* written in 1513 by an anonymous author known commonly as the translator of Livius, edited by John Lethbridge Kingsford.
9. *Ibid.*, *Henry V as Warlord*, Seward.
10. Juvénal des Ursins, Jean, Paris (1836), *Histoire de Charles VI*, ed. J.A. Buchon.
11. *Ibid.*, *Henry IV of England.*
12. *Ibid.*, *Henry V First English Life*, ed. Kingsford.
13. *Ibid.*, *The Chronicle of Adam of Usk*, A.D. 1377-1421, p. 168.
14. *Ibid.*, *Henry V as Warlord*, Desmond Seward.

Bibliography

Adam of Usk, *Chronica (1377-1421)* ed. E. Maunde Thompson, London, 1904.

Alnwick Castle Archives.

Armitage-Smith, S., *John of Gaunt*, London, 1904.

Aston, M.E., (Miss), *Thomas Arundel*, Oxford, 1967.

Bean, J.M.W., 'Henry IV and the Percies', *History*, XLIV, 1959.

Bevan, Bryan, *King Richard II*, London, 1990.

Bradley, Arthur Granville, *Owen Glyndwr*, 1902.

Bruce, Marie Louise, *The Usurper King*, London, 1986.

The Brut or the Chronicle of England, ed. F.W.D. Brie, Early English Text Society. Orig. Series, 136.

Burne, A.H., *The Battlefields of England*, 1950.

Butt, Ronald, *A History of Parliament: The Middle Ages, Henry IV*, 1989.

Capgrave, John, *The Chronicle of England*, ed. F.C. Hingeston, Rolls Series, 1958.

Chamberlin, E.R., *The Court of Virtue*, Cambridge Medieval History, Vol. VIII, 1965.

Chronique de la Traison et Mort de Richard II, ed. Benjamin Williams, 1846.

Clarke, M.V., *Fourteenth Century Studies*, ed. L.S. Sutherland and M. Mackisch, Oxford, 1937.

Créton, Jean, *Histoire du Roy d'Angleterre Richard*, ed. and trans. John Webb, 1824.

Daniel, Samuel, *The First Foure Bookes of the Civile Wars between the Two Houses of Lancaster and Yorke*, 1595.

Davies Chronicle of the Reigns of Richard II, Henry IV, ed. J.S. Davies, Camden Orig. Series 64, 1856.

Davies, R.G. and Denton, J.H. (eds.), *The English Parliament in the Middle Ages*, 1981.

English Historical Review (ed. Denys Hay, M.A.), No. CCCX, Jan. 1964.

Froissart, Jean, *Chroniques*, ed. K. Lettenhove, 1895.

Given-Wilson, Chris and Curteis, Alice, *The Royal Bastards of Medieval England*, 1985.

Goodman, Anthony, *John of Gaunt*, 1992.

Green, M.A. Everett (ed.), *Letters of Royal and Illustrious Ladies*, 1846.

Griffiths, W.R.M., 'The Military Career and *Affinity* of Henry Prince of Wales.' An unpublished Oxford University M.Litt. thesis, 1980.

Hallam, Elizabeth (ed.), *Plantagenet England*, 1990.

Hardyng Chronicle, Chronicle of John Hardyng, ed. Henry Ellis, 1812.

Harrison, Frank Llewellyn, *Music in Medieval Britain*, 1958.

Hayward, Sir John, *The First Part of the Life and Raigne of Henrie the Fourth*, 1599.

Hill, Sir Francis, *Medieval Lincoln*, 1990.

Holland, Bernard, *The Lancashire Hollands*, 1907.

Hingleston-Randolf, *Royal and Historical Letters of Henry IV*.

Huizinga, J., *The Waning of the Middle Ages*. First published 1924. Penguin reprint 1987.

Hutchison, H.F., *The Hollow Crown*, London, 1961.

Jacob, E.F., *The Fifteenth Century, 1399-1485*. Paperback edition 1992.

Kingsford, Lethbridge (ed.), *The First English Life of King Henry the Fifth*, written in 1513 by an anonymous author known commonly as the translator of Livius.

Kirby, J., *Henry IV of England*, 1970.

Lloyd, John Edward, *Owen Glendower*, 1992.

Morgan, Kenneth (ed.), *The Oxford Illustrated History of Britain*, 1952.

Monstrelet, Enguerrand de, *La Chronique*.

Radford, L.B., *Henry Beaufort*, 1908.

Seward, Desmond, *Henry V as Warlord*, 1987.

Shakespeare, William, *The Tragedy of Richard II*.

Shakespeare, William, *King Henry the Fourth*, Part I and II.

Skidmore, Ian, *Owain Glyndwr, Prince of Wales*. Paperback edition 1992.

Smith, Lucy Toulmin (ed.), *The Expeditions to Prussia and the Holy Land made by Henry Earl of Derby (afterwards King Henry IV) in the Years 1390-91 and 1392-93*.

Stow, John, *The Chronicles of England*, 1592.

Thomson, John A.F., *The Transformation of Medieval England, 1370-1529*. First published 1983.

Williams, G., *Owen Glendower*, 1966.

Wylie, J.H., *History of England under Henry IV*, 4 Vols., London, 1884-98.

Manuscripts

Harleian MSS 4579.

Harleian MSS 6829.

Harleian MSS 4380 (for Froissart illustrations).

Index